CONCILIUM

Religion in the Seventies

CONCILIUM

Concilium 123 (3/1979): Dogma

HEAVEN

Edited by
Bas van Iersel
and
Edward Schillebeeckx

THE SEABURY PRESS/NEW YORK

1979
The Seabury Press, 815 Second Avenue, New York, N.Y. 10017
ISBN: 0-8164-2231-1 (pbk.)   0-8164-0429-1

T. & T. Clark Ltd., 36 George Street, Edinburgh EH2 2LQ
ISBN: 0-567-30003-X (pbk.)

Library of Congress Catalog Card Number: 79-65694
Printed in the United States of America

CONTENTS

Editorial

THE FIRST Russian space flight returned to earth in 1961 and the commander, Yuri Gagarin, informed the world triumphantly: 'When we were up there, we met nobody'. Many Christians were, of course, astonished at this news—not because the Russians had not encountered the God of heaven or angels when they were in space, but because they had not expected the Soviet people to be so naïve. Even the most naïve believer knows intuitively that God is in heaven in a way that is different from that in which perceptible objects are in space.

This does not mean, however, that Christians are not embarrassed by the question of heaven. There is a great deal of embarrassment— sufficient for a whole number of *Concilium* to be devoted to it. The first article in this number, by Jan Kerkhofs, points clearly to the dimensions of this embarrassment. According to social surveys carried out in a number of countries, faith in heaven has decreased considerably, although less than belief in life after death and in hell. On the other hand, however, heaven is still one of the archetypes in the collective con- sciousness of most peoples and the concept still exercises an important influence on the Christian world of ideas. This has led to a good deal of tension and to feelings of uncertainty. This situation will undoubtedly persist for as long as the new symbols of faith are not universally accepted as the older ones were.

René Luneau's article serves as a contrapuntal accompaniment to this tune. It is clear from his analysis of a number of African traditions that these African peoples have no need of a concept such as that of heaven. For them, the dead are not cut off from life or the living. Generally speaking, the African believes that he dies to his childhood and youth when he is born again as an adult, that he later on dies to adult life in order to reinforce the little circle of wise old people and that he eventually joins the circle of revered ancestors when he dies as an old man.

Several of the authors who contribute to this number re-examine the biblical data about heaven. Jan Nelis, for example, goes into the age of the belief that God lived in heaven in the Old Testament. Yahweh is not called the God of heaven before the Persian period, although a God who lived in heaven is presupposed in a number of passages from the age of Israel's kings. The Israelite of that period certainly did not believe, however, that his dead went to that heaven. Enoch and Elijah were the exceptions that confirmed the rule.

Aelred Cody shows in his article how ideas about heaven gradually changed in the apocalyptic writings. Non-Jewish people were involved in the salvation of the end of time and, since less attention was given to a Jerusalem that was set free and restored and an Israel that was re-united as the place of salvation, the apocalyptic writers sometimes situated that salvation in God's heaven. Partly under the influence of the dualistic views of life and the world that prevailed in Hellenistic society, this idea of heaven as the place of salvation was quickly accepted in the early Christian communities. The Christian idea, however, had its own special characteristics because of the Christian emphasis on a present eschatology combined with faith in the resurrection of the dead.

In the light of these scriptural data, several authors take us further on in history. Peter Stockmeier examines the models of experience and the ideas that have arisen as a result of these scriptural data and shows how these models have at certain periods of history been dominant because they have reflected the current cultural or politico-economic ideas in a positive or a negative way. This thesis is fully confirmed by two outlines of experiences at a later period of history. The first of these outlines is provided by Robert Favre, who describes a literary expression of heaven that to a very great extent dominated eighteenth-century French civilization. The nineteenth-century American negro slaves were in many respects the complete opposite of the French educated classes of the preceding century and, in his article, James Cone outlines the meaning of heaven in their spirituals. What emerges from this study is much more than one would suspect simply from hearing these songs sung by a twentieth-century entertainer somewhere in the northern hemisphere.

The historically conditioned nature of the experiences and ideas that are connected with the concept of heaven runs through these three articles like a scarlet thread. In the same way, the last three contributions to this number of *Concilium* are characterised by the varying emphasis that they place on the Utopian aspect of heaven. Juan Luis de la Peña is concerned with the extent to which 'heaven' can be regarded as a projection and what this means for the nature and content of faith. Christian Duquoc tries to find an explanation for the remarkable separation of heaven from earth in the history of Christianity. He also checks a number of studies made by contemporary theologians against the New Testament statements, using his explanation as a background to this process of verification. He comes to the conclusion that it is as necessary to reject the negative statement that there is no heaven on earth as it is to reject the equally negative statement that there is no heaven with God. Finally, Stephen Happel discusses the conditions that must be satisfied if both the traditional and the new images of heaven are to be given a place in the faith of Christians who want to be faithful both to what has been handed down to them in the tradition of the Church and to their own rational thinking.

There are many reasons for keeping this editorial short, the most important being that most of the authors have written more than had originally been planned, with the result that the editors of this number have been directed back to the modest place where they belong. If a simple 'yes' or 'no' answer to the question of heaven has been avoided—and the editors believe that it has—and if heaven has not been made to die the death of a thousand qualifications—to quote, with Stephen Happel, the phrase used a long time ago by A. Flew[1]—then this is because the contributors have succeeded in their task.

BAS VAN IERSEL
EDWARD SCHILLEBEECKX

Note

1. This is how A. Flew concluded a story on pp. 96-97 of his and A. MacIntyre's *New Essays in Philosophical Theology* (London 1955).

Jan Kerkhofs

'Good Heavens'

THERE have been times in the past when theologians with a vivid imagination wrote detailed descriptions of heaven. Ths scriptural inspiration for this kind of description was often 'a new heaven and a new earth' (Rev. 21 : 1). Heaven itself was described as resting on the firmament that covered the flat disk of the earth. The sun, the moon and the stars revolved around the earth as mechanically as clockwork. God was enthroned above this heaven, which was divided into a complex hierarchy of spheres. These spheres were inhabited by those who had been made venerable and blessed and by the saints. There was also a scale depicted with angels, cherubs and powers, culminating in the Blessed Virgin in the last door of the upper heaven before the Holy Trinity. Matching this heaven (above) was a hell (below) with a corresponding hierarchy of zones of punishment, descending in order of severity. At the very bottom of this hierarchy of evil was the leader of the infernal angels, Lucifer.

The great theologians all knew, of course, that these representations of heaven (and hell) symbolised a mysterious reality. Even the great artists, poets, builders of cathedrals and workers in stained glass—Dante, van Eyck and Milton to name only three—as well as most of the ordinary people were able to distinguish, though some were more naïve than others, between the sign and its meaning when they 'saw' the realities of heaven, earth and hell interlaced in this way.

Even until quite recently, popular faith in the west was dominated by this vision. When life was often short, whole populations were from time to time decimated by epidemics and death was encountered in the midst of life, heaven and hell were tangible realities in the collective consciousness of western man.[1] It is, however, true to say that hell-fire sermons were commoner in popular preaching than descriptions of

1

heavenly peace and the reminder that, at death, *in paradisum te deducant angeli* was not always able to overcome fear of purgatory, damnation and hell. This is clear from the frequently attested desire to gain indulgences (such as those granted to pilgrims to the Portiuncula and elsewhere) and the saying of numerous masses. (Christians in the higher income bracket were able to take out a kind of posthumous insurance policy by having masses said for the repose of their souls.)

This classical familiarity with heaven (and hell) has become less unquestionably accepted now, in the second half of the twentieth century. It is almost impossible to investigate scientifically the extent to which really fundamental changes have taken place in the faith of the ordinary people, partly because no comparative opinion polls have been made. Nonetheless, we may claim with some safety that the naïvety with which our ancestors believed in heaven has obviously disappeared. This is to some extent because faith in heaven has decreased with the rapid spread of secularisation and its accompanying phenomenon of pervasive scientific doubt. It has, however, almost entirely disappeared also partly because the new symbols for the 'heavenly reality' have not yet been recognised as such. The 'new angels'[2] have not yet been sufficiently studied and, as in other spheres of life, many people have suspended judgment. In the case of heaven too, it is possible to speak of a 'homeless mind',[3] even though millions of Europeans refer to heaven every day when they use such phrases as 'good heavens' in their own languages.[4]

1. HEAVEN IN PUBLIC OPINION

According to a summary of five surveys of public opinion on religious convictions carried out in fifteen different countries between 1947 and 1975, it is clear that faith in God is still widespread and relatively unchanged.[5] What also emerges from this article is that fewer people believe in a life after death and that this number is probably going to continue to decrease. It would, however, perhaps be more correct to speak in this context of a process of polarisation. It is evident from a comparative survey conducted in the U.S.A. that those who doubt the reality of a life after death and the existence of the devil tend to be non-believers—possibly because public opinion has become more tolerant in this sphere—whereas the number of believers who accept these date is fairly constant.[6] In the 21-31 age group, there was a clear decrease between 1957 and 1968 in belief in a life after death (that is, a decrease from 75·4 per cent to 70·7 per cent) and in the devil (from 69·5 per cent to 58·9 per cent), whereas there was an increase in the 76+ age group, from 75 per cent to 82·6 per cent and from 52·1 per cent to 60 per cent respectively.[7]

With regard to heaven and hell, the only internationally comparative data that are available are from 1968. They have to be used with a great deal of caution. This Gallup poll of 1968 produced the following results in respect of belief in heaven, a life after death, reincarnation and hell. The figures are percentages.

	Heaven			Life after Death			Reincarnation			Hell		
	Yes	No	Don't Know	Yes	No	Don't Know	Yes	No	Don't Know	Yes	No	Don't Know
1. Austria	44	49	7	38	56	6	20	73	7	26	68	6
2. Great Britain	45	27	19	38	35	27	18	52	30	23	58	19
3. Finland	62	20	18	55	23	22	—	—	—	29	49	22
4. France	39	52	9	35	53	12	23	62	15	22	70	8
5. Greece (Athens)	65	23	12	57	28	15	22	60	18	62	25	13
6. Netherlands	54	31	15	50	35	15	10	55	35	28	61	11
7. Norway	60	20	20	54	25	21	14	57	29	36	45	19
8. Sweden	43	42	15	38	47	15	12	72	16	17	71	12
9. Switzerland	50	41	9	50	41	9	—	—	—	25	67	8
10. U.S.A.	85	11	4	73	19	8	20	64	16	65	29	6
11. West Germany	43	42	15	41	45	14	25	54	21	25	62	13

From almost all the surveys what emerges is a degree of incoherence (although surveys at a deeper level might possibly reveal greater coherence). One fairly clear conclusion that can be drawn, however, is that belief in heaven is stronger than belief in life after death and that belief in the latter is stronger than belief in hell. The results also give the impression that belief in heaven is weaker in the sociologically Protestant countries of Europe than it is in the sociologically Catholic countries. There are, however, several exceptions. In the Netherlands, for instance, members not only of the Calvinist-Zwinglian Reformed Churches, but also those of the Lutheran Reformed Church have a stronger faith in a life after death than Catholics. This is in striking contrast to the situation in Great Britain and West Germany. One is bound to ask in this context whether this difference has come about as a result of differences between the Catholic and the Protestant theologies of immortality or the resurrection, in which the Protestant doctrine of *sola fides* has led to a radical distinction having been made between immortality and the resurrection.[8]

There are also striking differences between northern and sociologically Protestant countries such as Norway and Finland and southern European and sociologically Catholic countries such as Italy. Belief in heaven would seem to be more pronounced in the north than in the south, where, for example, 41·5 per cent of the population of Leghorn in 1977 believed in paradise and 38·6 per cent believed in hell.[9] Even in Rome, there was a lower score for belief in heaven than in Norway or Finland.[10] Generally speaking, practising Christians, both Protestant and Catholic, have greater faith in life after death, heaven and hell than non-practising believers. Women also believe more strongly in heaven and a life after death than men. Whether younger people believe more or less than older people in heaven, hell or life after death or whether the better educated believe more or less than the less well educated varies from country to country.

Most of the surveys have been carried out in the U.S.A., where it appears that faith in God is much stronger than belief in a life after death, which is in turn weaker than belief in heaven. From the overall sociological point of view, it is interesting to note that, in the so-called Christian countries, belief in heaven is much stronger in the U.S.A. than in any other country and that more American Protestants believe in heaven than Catholics. With regard to belief in a life after death, Lawrence M. Hynson Jnr. has confirmed that 'most people still adhere to a belief in an afterlife. Sects register the highest percentage of believers (84 per cent), followed by Protestants (76 per cent), Catholics (72 per cent), no religion (39 per cent) and Jews (17 per cent)'.[11]

It is also interesting to note that between 10 and 25 per cent of the population of the so-called Christian West believe in reincarnation. There is some evidence from surveys in Denmark of a rapid increase in this belief, especially among young people, no doubt influenced by Eastern religions.

It is clear from the sociological material at our disposal that we must be extremely cautious in expressing universal judgments about trends in public opinion in this matter. P. Delooz has pointed, in an excellent study,[12] to the incoherence of the responses to questions about the 'invisible' realities. The following results were obtained from an IFOP survey carried out in 1958 among young French adults aged between 18 and 30 and other surveys undertaken in Italy (1970) and Belgium (1969):

belief in God	73%
belief in the divinity of Christ	62%
belief in an afterlife	55%
belief in the influence of this life on the next	46%
belief in heaven, purgatory and hell	38%
belief in the resurrection of the body	32%

2. HEAVEN IN THE RELIGION OF THE PEOPLE

Despite the changes that have undoubtedly taken place in our belief in heaven, both with regard to the form and the firmness of that conviction, heaven is still one of the established archetypes in the collective consciousness of most peoples. Almost every historical study of comparative religions has shown that the firmament is the symbol of the 'highest' reality, the 'unattainable' and the 'infinite depths'. It is not in general possible to establish whether this reality is a person, a perspective or a projection. According to the Greeks, heaven was a kind of upper deck above the rest of creation, which consisted of many decks.

The same can be said of the religion of the people in Hinduism, Buddhism, later Judaism and Islam and of the religion of the Indians of North and South America. In many cases, heaven and earth are believed to be connected by the top and the roots of the 'tree of life'. Fruitfulness comes (through the rain and the sun) from heaven, as does the spirit (through the wind). Heaven reveals the strangeness of the deity (in the tempest and bad weather). It contains also many divine cryptograms (in the stars).

Many primitive peoples believe that heaven is the symbol of the male principle and that earth symbolises the female element. In China, heaven has traditionally been the place where the spirits live. It is also the symbol of divine power and possibly also of the power of the people and the emperor, thus hypostasising the collective consciousness of the people. Did not Mao Tse Tung call women 'the other half of heaven'? In the classical teaching of Confucianism, heaven was both the personal deity (during the Chou dynasty predominantly) and earth's partner in a marriage from which the universe came (under the influence of the ideas of yin and yang). The worship of heaven was reserved for the emperor, who never, however, became a real incarnation of the deity. The relationship between immanence and transcendence was different in the Chinese view of the world from that which prevailed in the western world-view. It is, for example, clear from the structure of the Temple of Heaven in Peking that there was a conviction among the Chinese of continuity between the divine and the human worlds that was not traditionally present in the West, where Christian churches were built with towers and spires pointing towards heaven.[13]

In all of the six great world-religions of today (Hinduism, Buddhism, Zoroastrianism, Judaism, Islam and Christianity), there is some sort of belief in a kind of resurrection and in heaven as a place of fulfilment and greater life. This is in striking contrast to the religion of the ancient Greeks, who thought of man's continued life as a shadowy existence (in Hades) and to many of the primitive animistic religions of Africa, in which cult of ancestors is less explicitly a belief in heaven.[14] Heaven is central in the sacred writings of India, the Koran and the Christian scriptures. A relatively short period of rationalism in the West, from the eighteenth to the twentieth centuries, has, moreover, been followed by a phase in which many forms of belief in 'another life' are flourishing. Many people in the post-Christian West are now trying to make heaven an experience of the present within a monistic view of the world by using artificial means such as drugs, yoga, transcendental meditation and religious sexual practices.[15] Many others have suspended judgment and claim that they are agnostics with regard to heaven.

Indeed, we may say that man has never succeeded rationally in solving the mystery of death and has therefore not been able to deal with the mystery of heaven, which has sometimes been de-symbolised as a nirvana and at others has been seen as the end-product of a long series of reincarnations, in the sense of phases of purification or the incomprehensible consequence of a blind process of predestination.

It is possible that we can gain a clearer impression from the thoughts and feelings of the dying themselves of what heaven may be like—they should, at least, be able to provide us with a sense of direction. As far as I know, no systematic study has ever been undertaken with this aim in view. C. S. Lewis has, however, described what seems to be a fairly widespread experience: 'There was a sudden clearing of his eyes . . . he saw Them . . . The dim consciousness of friends about him which had haunted his solitudes from infancy was now at last explained; that central music in every pure experience which had always just evaded memory was now at last recovered . . . He saw not only Them, he saw Him . . . cool light . . . clarity itself'.[16] Heaven is presented in this description as a luminous, depersonalised space, filled with the essential elements of personal beings and with the being of God himself, interwoven and yet distinct. It can be compared with the apocalyptic description (Rev. 22). At the same time, it also contains a longing for wholeness and cosmic freedom. Heaven is a place where the whole universe is ultimately accommodated, everyone is at home and no one, not even the devil, is lost. In this way, Lewis' description is similar to the doctrine of apokatastasis of several of the Greek Fathers of the Church.

In a hedonistic way, this primordial dream is also often closely associated in the consciousness of the people with a collective memory[17] of a paradise on earth and with an expectation of a heavenly Jerusalem of one kind or another. Although several books and articles have been published on the sociology of the dreams of the people,[18] it would be valuable to have a more extensive bibliography at our disposal. There have always been periods in history in which millenarianism and messianism have been rife and this memory and expectation have therefore been kept alive in the collective consciousness of the people. It would certainly seem as though man cannot live without some hope in heaven and that he has to express this hope in images of a perfect beginning and a perfect end. (Many fairy-tales, films, plays and ballets express this very clearly.) Heaven is, in other words, the image of man's desire for happiness and the symbol of what is positive in life. 'Blessed' and 'heavenly' are often used synonymously.

Many of the elements contained in man's collective consciousness—if not all of those elements—have for centuries provided the West with basically Christian ideas and images and this process has not ceased. The word 'heaven', for instance, occurs in many everyday expressions: 'good heavens', 'to be in the seventh heaven', 'in heaven's name', 'it was heaven on earth', 'heaven only knows where it is' and so on. Heaven sometimes indicates a superlative: 'to cry out to heaven (for vengeance)', 'a heavenly experience (day, etc.)' or 'he moved heaven and earth'. Heaven almost always expresses some kind of perfection and often points to a surprising, unknown or entirely different element. Sometimes only the element of surprise is expressed, as in 'good heavens' and at others the words are used to express an extreme emphasis: 'I wish to heaven that . . .' of 'for heaven's sake'. There are, of course, many other examples.

Heaven, of course, has always been connected in the Christian collective consciousness in some way or another with the state of being with God. Nonetheless, the tangible social aspects seem always to have predominated. Heaven is a place where no one suffers from hunger, for example—one eats with a golden spoon. (It should not be forgotten in this context that for centuries whole populations in Europe lived at subsistence level, as the inhabitants of the Sahel do today.) Lovers will be re-united in heaven. (We have a certain number of books and articles devoted to epitaphs, but it would be useful if there were a complete socio-historical analysis of this theme.[19]) There will be no more war and death will have no more power over us. Everything will be beautiful and everyone will be young, sensible and attractive. This list could be extended, but it may be terminated with a comment on the Christian attitude to sexuality in heaven—unlike, for example, Indian Hindus, Christians have not known what to do about this phenomenon.

3. THE CRISIS IN OUR IMAGINATION OF HEAVEN

As G. van Hemert has correctly pointed out, 'One of the main reasons why there is a crisis in our imagination of heaven is undoubtedly because the idea that God is 'above' us has only in our own time ceased to be valid. A direct consequence of the Copernican world-view and the teachings of Galileo and Newton was that the idea of a higher world where God, the angels and the saints lived lost its status. This, however, only very gradually penetrated into the depths of people's feelings and even then was not fully assimilated until the later revolution in our world-view, brought about by Darwin's evolutionary understanding of history as an ascending line, began to take effect. In our own time, we are confronted with the need to take both the universe, of which our planet, earth, is not the centre, and evolution, in the biological sense of the world, seriously into account in imagining faith, hope and love'.[20]

For centuries, heaven was the keystone of the cosmic order. It was a fixed point above time that passed. It was the perspective of a lasting infinity, in striking contrast to the finite world of history which was always eluding men's grasp. It was also an escape from the *samsara* of man's destiny, with its cycle of changes. This heaven can no longer be used as a symbol of space and time and a new symbol is necessary for a reality that must be re-defined.

Paul Ricoeur has said: 'Even if we modern men are no longer able to experience sacred symbolism in accordance with the original faith, we can at least try, in and through criticism, to find a later naïvety'.[21] An increasingly intense search is therefore being made for experiences of heaven within our existence on earth. This is being done not because there is no 'heaven', but rather because this heaven cannot be displaced 'upwards', 'forward' or 'backwards' (as a memory of paradise in the past). Many people are looking for experiences of eternity or happiness in their own existence or in their life with others. Some have found this type of experience in love and other aspects of life with their fellow-men, in accordance with the idea that the kingdom of God is among us, in all kinds of experience involving an extension of consciousness or by means of a renewal through the Holy Spirit of the kind that takes place in the charismatic movement and in various sects.

It looks, then, as though very many people today are finding the rationalistic world-view unsatisfactory and are therefore in search of supra-rational experiences of happiness and identity, for the most part outside the sphere of institutional religion. Rationalism clearly went counter to the indifference of the churches (an indifference that was often tinged with pessimism) and tried to educate 'terrorised' man by encouraging him to believe in life here and now and in progress and, more recently, by making a direct attack against death through medicine and the public health service. Under the influence of rationalism, we no longer give way to what has been called the Catholic 'distaste for life' and 'holy longing for death'.[22] Many people are now trying to find a heavenly experience within an existence that has in many respects remained deathly and has in many places given rise to a pre-Christian pessimism.

My outline of the situation is, of course, too condensed and therefore lacking in light and shade. It is obvious that what we urgently need is a whole series of psychological and sociological studies devoted to the recent changes that have taken place in the attitude of western man towards life and death. Studies of this kind ought also to form part of an investigation on an even grander scale into the changes in value-concepts and forms of human experience. In the meantime, however, several

studies have appeared in recent years and these contain valuable information and insights. We shall consider some of these now.

Man's imaginative powers and thought are to some extent determined
by time and space. His experience or expectation of happiness or unhappiness is expressed not only in categories of time, but also in concepts and
images of space. In his book, *Honest to God*, published more than
twenty-five years ago, John A. T. Robinson rejected the 'crudely spatial'
view of heaven contained in the Bible, but nonetheless reverted to spatial
language when he spoke of heaven as the 'ground' of existence. Van
Niftrik suggested that heaven was an 'interiorised space' and that God
was the one who enlarges space and contains all things. Heaven, he
claimed, was 'the space of God's love for men'.[23] The churches, temples
and the whole expanse of nature were, in his opinion, the symbols of that
space. Clearly, van Niftrik was emphasising space—the space of God and
all men for all men and all things—encounter—the encounter between
God and men— and confrontation—the over and against that definitively
eludes history. For him and many other Christians, heaven is not simply a
vague place beyond this world—on the other side of the dark river of
death—but the God of love himself. In that love men encounter each
other.

Other scholars who have examined this question have come to the
conclusion that the spatial representations of heaven and hell are social
functions of the collective consciousness. According to B. P. Prusak, for
example,[24] heaven and hell were originally expressions of protest against
social and political injustice, so that they are in a sense similar to the
protest made in the present-day theologies of liberation. It was from this
social and political protest movement that the need arose to create
spheres of heaven and hell, as places of reward and punishment respectively, in accordance with the demands of justice. This was in the first
place a social need, but it later became privatised and was applied to the
personal salvation or damnation of individuals. The messianic kingdom
and man's apocalyptic expectations are fundamentally collective realities
and Prusak therefore wonders whether hell was not really a 'Christian'
way of taking revenge and heaven and hell were not primarily, at least
from the historical point of view, social ways of creating a community with
a sense of responsibility, with the ultimate aim of survival.

According to other scholars, it is essential for us to believe in heaven,
with a faith that has been purified, but is nonetheless authentic, if our
earth is to remain inhabitable and man is to be set free from his deathly
seriousness. Heaven enables us to recognise earth as a space for a comedy
which is both human and divine and which is constantly transcended by a
drama of love.[25]

Van Hemert and others have tried to solve this problem by looking for the roots of man's existence outside time in a state in which he can share in what Teilhard de Chardin called the 'divine milieu' and in which experiences of the permanence of interpersonal faithfulness are expressions of God's faithfulness here and now and his will to remain faithful to man beyond death.

It is possible that the only way of elaborating this view is by following a personalistic course, developing the early distinctions between *tempus*, *aevum* and *aeternitas* or between *chronos* and *kairos* and systematically investigating all the many aspects of man's experience of time and space.[26] It might also be very instructive to study various aspects of the death of a number of privileged witnesses.

To conclude this article, I would like to point briefly to the symbols of love and light as necessarily replacing all spatial and even all ethical images (of reward and punishment). This desire was expressed emphatically by Saint Teresa of Avila in her well-known statement: 'I would like to destroy hell and heaven so that God might be really loved for himself alone'.

Translated by David Smith

Notes

1. Philippe Ariès *L'homme devant la mort* (Paris 1977) p. 642.
2. Peter L. Berger *A Rumour of Angels. Modern Society and the Rediscovery of the Supernatural* (New York 1969).
3. Peter L. Berger and others *The Homeless Mind. Modernization and Consciousness* (New York 1973).
4. For example: 'juste ciel', 'bon ciel', 'lieve hemel', 'gerechter Himmel' and so on.
5. Lee Seligman 'Multi-nation Surveys of Religious Beliefs' in *Journal for the Scientific Study of Religion* 16, 3 (1977) pp. 289-294.
6. A. Greeley *National Catholic Reporter*, 3 February 1978, p. 6, correctly commented: 'Forty years ago, the first time such a question was asked was in a national survey, 70 per cent of the American population believed in life after death. Seventy per cent still believe in it. . . . For a decline in religious devotion and religious authority there is plenty of evidence, but a decline in religion (fairly enough measured, I think, by belief in human survival), there is no shred of evidence.'
7. Bradley R. Hertel and Hart M. Nelson 'Are we entering a post-Christian Era? Religious Belief and Attendance in America, 1957-1968' *Journal for the Scientific Study of Religion* 13, 4 (1974) pp. 409-419. These authors have concluded: 'From our own analysis we conclude that, while candour in expressing disbelief appeared to be on the rise in America by the late 1960s, the proportion of Americans who continue to believe in the major tenets of Christianity is not changing dramatically. We wish to close by noting that what is needed now is research into the *qualitative* dimension of orthodoxy to determine the nature of what is believed, and in particular whether or not believers accept "devil", "afterlife", etc., as having transcendental referents' (p. 418).
8. G. Greshake and G. Lohfink *Naherwartung, Auferstehung, Unsterblichkeit. Untersuchungen zur chrislichen Eschatologie* (Friegurg 1975).
9. S. Burga lassi *Il Regno—Attualità* (Bologna 10, 1978) p. 204.
10. E. Pin and C. Cavallin *Attegiamenti religiosi ed ateizzanti dei Romani* (Rome 1970).
11. Lawrence M. Hynson Jnr. 'Religion, Attendance and Belief in an Afterlife' *Journal for the Scientific Study of Religion* 14, 3 (1975) pp. 285-287. The percentages given here are for 1973 (Roper Public Opinion Research Center Study No. 9002).
12. Pierre Delooz 'Who Believes in the Hereafter?', in *Death and Presence (The Psychology of Death and the Afterlife), Studies in the Psychology of Religion*, ed. A. Godin, *Lumen Vitae* V (Brussels 1972) pp 17-38.
13. The 'Middle Kingdom' (= China) is also called the 'Heavenly Kingdom' and is inhabited by 'heavenly beings' (= Chinese). For the various meanings of heaven in Confucianism, see Julia Chang, *Confucianism and Christianity. A Comparative Study* (Tokyo and New York 1977).
14. M. Singleton 'Ancestors, Adolescents and the Absolute' *Pro Mundi Vita*, Bulletin No. 68 (1977).

15. C. Y. Glock and R. N. Bellah, eds. *The New Religious Consciousness* (Berkeley and London 1976). A fundamental study of horoscopes would be valuable.

16. C. S. Lewis *The Screwtape Letters* (London 1943) pp. 156-158. Similar experiences have been described by Hans Urs bon Balthasar *Herrlichkeit* I, II and III (Einsiedeln 1961-1969).

17. Mircea Eliade *La nostalgie des origines. Méthodologie et histoire des religions* (Paris 1971); H. Desroche *Sociologies religieuses* (Paris 1968). There is also the myth of paradise in the so-called American dream and the myth of holidays 'in paradise'; see J. Gritti 'Le paradis en miettes' *La Vie Spirituelle* 30-38 (1977).

18. H. Desroche *Les dieux rêvés* (Paris 1972); *ibid. Sociologie de l'espérance* (Paris 1973); see also Arnold Toynbee, Arthur Koestler and others *Life after Death* (London 1976). For Islam, see El-Saleh (Soubhi) *La vie selon le Coran* (Paris 1971), who discusses the difficulties of the Muslim theologians with the popular ideas of heaven. See also R. Laurentin *Nouvelles dimensions de l'espérance* (Paris 1972); P. Versins *Encyclopédie de l'Utopie et de la Science Fiction* (Lausanne 1972); R. Caillois, G. E. von Grunebaum, eds. *Le rêve et les sociétés humaines* (Paris 1967). See also R. Bastide's well-known *Sociologie du rêve*.

19. G. Vovelle and M. Vovelle *Vision de la mort et de l'au-delà en Provence d'après les autels des âmes du purgatoire, XV-XX^esiècles* (Paris 1970); see also J. Ntedika *L'évocation de l'au-delà dans la prière pour les morts. Etude de patristique et de liturgies latines* (IVe-VIIIe s.) (Louvain 1971). This second work was published in the series *Recherches Africaines de Théologie. Travaux de la Faculté de Théologie de l'Université Lovanium de Kinshasa*, 2.

20. G. van Hemert *Lieve Hemel. Denken over het komende bij beelden die verdwijnen* (Bilthoven 1975); B. van Onna 'Paradijstoestand en evolutie' *Concilium* 3 (1967) pp. 126-135.

21. *La symbolique du mal* (Paris 1960); English translation: *The Symbolism of Evil* (Boston 1972) p. 351.

22. Robert Favre *La more dans la littérature et la pensée françaises au siècle des lumières* (Lyon 1978) p. 147.

23. G. C. van Niftrik *De Hemel. Over de ruimtelijkheid van God* (Nijkerk 1968) p. 49.

24. Bernard P. Prusak 'Heaven and Hell: Eschatological Symbols of Existential Protest' *Cross Currents* XXIV, 4 (1975) pp 475-491.

25. See Peter L. Berger *The Precarious Vision. A Sociologist Looks at Social Fictions and Christian Faith* (New York 1961) p. 214: 'From the Christian point of view one can say that comedy, unlike tragedy, bears within it a great secret. This secret is the promise of redemption. For redemption promises in eternity what comedy gives us in its few moments of precarious liberation—the collapse of the walls of our imprisonment. . . . There will be no tragedy in heaven. . . . The tragic shows us man in time, but the comic may well give us an intimation of what man is and always will be, even in eternity'.

26. F. Russo 'La parapsychologie' *Etudes* 349 (1978) pp. 7-26.

René Luneau

What can the African Traditions tell us about the Hereafter?

IN ANY article about religion in black Africa, it is most important to bear in mind that the continent is three times as large as Europe and that it contains more than a thousand ethnic groups of varying importance, all with different traditions and ways of life. (Three examples of very divergent ways of life are those of the forest-dweller, the peasant inhabiting the savannah and the herdsman.) In addition, each ethnic group is subjected in the present century to an inescapable, but in each case different, process of change.

With these differences in mind, it should be easily recognised that nothing that I say in this article can be applied indiscriminately to the whole of the continent. All that I can do here is to point to the idea that certain ethnic groups in Africa, which I have selected from a very wide possible choice, have of what we call the 'hereafter'. Clearly, it would hardly be possible, within the limits imposed by this short article to do more than provide a very broad outline of the most important traditional African ideas about the hereafter. I cannot, in other words, support my statements by detailed evidence of the data that have been observed. The reader who would like to go further into any aspect of the African attitude towards the hereafter should consult the very full bibliography available.[1]

Let me say at once that this hereafter is not 'heaven'. The Africans do not equate the hereafter with heaven in the way that we understand it in our western Christian tradition. This does not mean that they know nothing about heaven or that they attach no importance to it. According to many African myths, it is in heaven that God seeks refuge after a tiring and difficult period of association with men.[2]

13

Among the Dangaleat of Chad, for example, heaven and God are equated in religious language, as though, as J. Fédry has said, 'man's empirical experience of the vault of heaven—its circumference is everywhere and its centre nowhere and the horizon is wherever the viewer may be standing and, wherever he is, he is always at the centre—symbolises the experience of a presence that encompasses and yet goes beyond man and at the same time gives him rain, life and death'. It is clear, then, that heaven is not entirely absent from African religious experience. It is inaccessible, but the tangible sign of God's transcendence. According to a Dagba myth in Central Africa, 'a rope, a very big rope' originally connected heaven to earth, but because of the foolishness of the first man to live on earth God pulled up the rope. This rope is now 'the Milky Way that can be seen when heaven is clear'. God thus removed himself from men and those who die cannot go to heaven.

Why should they in any case go to heaven if they are African? The traditional Christian teaching, according to which heaven and God's presence are the culmination of a life of faith, is not meaningful to Africans, who have never received any revelation about the abode of the dead. Basing their thinking on their own traditional wisdom, they certainly question themselves fundamentally about death and the grief that accompanies it, but at the same time they believe that death cannot be dissociated from life and that it is the hidden face of its mystery. If, on the one hand, it is true that it represents a radical break with life, they have the consolation of knowing that man's task is to learn about it, as a phenomenon that is very closely tied to every stage of his development. The African has to die to his childhood in order to become a man. He has to die to the adult world in order to acquire the privileges of old age. Finally, he has to die to old age in order to enter the realm of his ancestors. He has, in other words, to die many times if he wants to live and nothing is more important than life.

Is it, however, possible to say that the dead live? According to the popular wisdom of Zaire, 'just as a jar pours out its water when it is broken, so too does a man pour out his life when he dies'.[3] This idea of the jar breaking figures frequently in African funeral rites in forms that express, often very forcibly, the radical break that occurs at death. For example, the handle is removed from the hoe of the Bambara peasant in Mali before he is buried. He is dressed in all his clothes, but they are put on inside out and the cord of his trousers is tied at the back. The little gourd from which water was poured around the outside of his tomb is broken.[4] Elsewhere in Africa, the house of the man who has just died is deserted and, if he is the chief of a village, the whole population leaves the village.[5]

Everywhere in Africa, death is regarded as an essential part of the human condition—according to a Fon proverb, 'death is linked to the day of birth'—but why it should occur here and now cannot be explained. Death as such does not surprise the African, but a particular death may cause scandal. Even if God is ultimately responsible for everything, the African always looks for convincing reasons—not just biological ones—for such a death. Almost the only deaths which do not cause surprise in Africa are those of old people. All other cases of death are followed by long soothsaying sessions.

The strange practice of questioning the dead is widespread among the Casamance in Angola. In this, the deceased is thought to impart to those who are carrying the litter on which his body is lying certain strictly codified movements which can be recognised as affirmative or negative answers to the questions that he is asked. Such questions are, for example, whether his death was intended by God, whether it was a just punishment imposed because of an offence committed, whether it was the result of an act of revenge or whether it was the work of a sorcerer.[6]

Death brings so much grief that it has to be exorcised in some way. This exorcism is accomplished when the reason for this particular person's death is known. In addition, everything is done to keep death at a distance. It is, for example, forbidden among certain peoples to speak about it.[7] Mourning is often accompanied by elaborate rituals and the surviving partner of a marriage is obliged to live for months outside the village community. The gravediggers and those who have taken part in the funeral ceremony or the burial have to be purified. The deceased is frequently the object of prayers and rituals so that he will not haunt the people of his house. Almost everywhere in black Africa, such practices are found in one form or another, according to the local traditions, and there are many others in addition. No attempt is made to treat death lightly. It cuts men off and cannot be forgiven. According to the Fon, 'there is no sacrifice for death'.[8]

What is paradoxical in the African view of death is that, although it is regarded as a violent break with life, there is no total discontinuity between what has taken place in the past and what is to happen in the future. This attitude can be observed in many African traditions connected with death. In Benin, for example, when a king dies, he is said to have 'gone to Alada'. Alada is the source of the Benin royalty. The dead king returns there to be 'among his equals'. In the same way, a deceased soothsayer is also said to have 'gone to Ife', the religious centre of soothsaying by the fá.[9]

No attempt is made to minimise the harshness of the event or the radical break that it causes, but it is contained within the continuity of a worldly tradition. Certain forms of behaviour that appear strange at first sight can be understood if this attitude to tradition is borne in mind. A frequent practice at a funeral is for the mourners to entrust certain gifts—trousers, a loin cloth or money in small change—to the keeping of the dead person, who has the task of handing the gifts on to those who have already died before him and whom he is about to join. According to a quite common oral tradition, the dead live underground, although this abode is sometimes thought to be beyond the hills and far from the familiar environment. This village of the dead is often very similar to those of the living and, if the myths are to be believed, they have sometimes been visited by travellers. The Bobo peasants from Upper Volta, for example, in despair because there was no millet in their own market, believed that 'only the market of the dead still has customers. Poor people do not hesitate to go to Hokani—the place-name that points to the hereafter'.[10] There is also the familiar story of the man who died several years ago and whom 'someone' has met in a distant village which no one has ever visited, but whose name is well known.

This consciousness of the continuity that exists between life on earth and the hereafter extends beyond the realm of anecdotes. According to a fine Fon funeral chant from Benin, the deceased 'has crossed the mirror; for him, nothing will exist any longer in the darkness'. The image of the 'mirror' is an excellent one, but the important aspect of this statement is that a crossing is possible. The whole African tradition bears witness to the conviction that death is a threshold opening the way to a new 'birth' and that it has to be experienced as a continuous initiation.

Certain apparently strange practices can be understood in the light of this conviction that death is a process of initiation. For example, among the Batabwa of Zaire, a man suffers and dies back to back with a woman sitting on her heels with her legs wide apart, as though it were her task to give birth to him again.[11] At a Sar funeral in Chad, dancers follow the same rhythms and movements as those performed in dances of initiation (*nganjang*). According to M. Fournier, 'the use of these nganjang rhythms not only revives the memory of the past, but also points to an understanding both of the initiation and of the death that are being experienced, not as a single, individual event at the end of one human life, but as a social phenomenon in which the life of the dead person who is being initiated into new life is united with the whole community of those who have disappeared'.[12] Among the Sar, 'there is no opposition between death and life. Life is the all-embracing totality and there is no need to speak about it. Yo—death—is fully integrated into life and the total experience of the life of the group goes beyond the dying of individuals'.[13] According to this understanding of death, man goes from threshold to threshold and from initiation to initiation throughout his life. Biological death is only one threshold among others and it opens the way into the world of the ancestors.

This conviction of continuity between this world and the next is so strong that the two worlds are frequently seen as the same reality. Among the Bazela of Zaire, three stages are recognised in the process of social integration. These are childhood (*bwàna*), adulthood (*butamè*) and old age (*bukùlù*). It is possible that these three stages of life are no more than a poor reproduction of the primordial structure prevailing in the other world. In order to acquire the status of ancestor in the hereafter, it is necessary to cross three stages. Each of these stages corresponds to a particular ceremony in the funeral rites. These stages are spread, as are the ceremonies marking them, over more than a year. The first is *bumufwè*, when the man has just died and has crossed the threshold. The second is *bumufù*, the time of uncertainty when it is not known whether those whom he has just left will regard him as worthy to achieve the dignity of an ancestor or whether they will reject him as responsible for the misfortunes and the bad omens that have followed his death. The third stage is that of *busyèkùlù*. The virtue of a special rite known as *muumbu*, which means literally 'greeting the arrival of the dead person', makes it possible for the deceased to be called an ancestor and to become the object of veneration by those who belong to his family. When this stage has been reached, signs are sought for his return in one of the children who has been or is going to be born.

This, however, is not the whole story. The ancestors are chosen on the basis of criteria which express the values and practices in which the group is able to recognise itself. In this way, they constitute a hierarchy that is closely parallel to that of the group itself in this world. The first members of this hierarchy are the ancestors who were the first-born and therefore the founders of the ethnic group in question. These are the *inkolwe*. These are followed by the anonymous ancestors, the *basyekùlù* or 'early sons', whose names have been forgotten in the course of generations. Finally, there are those who are called the near ancestors, 'our fathers' (*batātà bētu*) or 'our great fathers' (*ba nkambò bètu*), with whom the ancestral relationship is closest. In this hierarchy of ancestral lineage, each ancestor occupies the place that he occupied when he was living on earth.

What is true for the Bazela[14] also applies, *mutatis mutandis*, to very many other ethnic groups in Africa. This is the case even if the presence of the dead in daily life goes far beyond the frontiers of an officially recognised cult of ancestors.

It would, of course, be quite wrong to regard these elaborate constructions of the collective mind of the people simply as a product of the imagination and not related in any way to the reality of life. In many parts of black Africa, the dead are not simply remembered—they are also often guests in the home. Among the Fon of Benin, for example, one of the huts in the family enclosure belongs to the *asānyì*, which are 'metal objects planted in the ground and symbolising the deceased'.[15] According to R. M. Segbenou, 'every deceased person whose funeral rites have been completed has an *asānyì* and this is usually regarded as the deceased person himself. The *àjàlásá*, the special meeting place of the members (of the extended family) is often built opposite the hut belonging to these *asānyì*. The close proximity of these two huts points to the close tie between the living and the dead. The meetings take place in front of the ancestors or rather, they take place with the ancestors. These ancestors are also able to speak through the fá or oracle'.[16] With this phenomenon in mind, it is not difficult to understand R. Bastide's observation made a decade ago: 'The civilisations of Africa are symbiotic civilisations in which the dead and the living form a single community. This is easy because death is regarded simply as a superior status'.[17]

In addition to speaking through the medium of the fá or soothsayer, the dead also visit earth and make their will known to men through dreams. An example of this application of the dream is found among the Tetela of Zaire. 'In order to settle an important and difficult case of justice, the leaders of the community began by withdrawing and dreaming about it. The ancestors then came to tell them who was right and who was wrong.'[18] Closely related to this practice is that of the trance, in which the ancestor is able for a time to possess the one whom he has chosen and make his will known to others through that intermediary.[19]

In Africa, the dead are too important to be forgotten. If it is true that death as an initiation is directed towards life, then we are bound to recognise that the dead are in many ways more alive than the living themselves. It should also be borne in mind that many of the dead have not reached their ultimate destiny. The Tetela of Zaire and other ethnic groups, for example, believe that an ancestor is able to return in a child, in obedience to certain very complicated rules, in which an essential part is played by the sequence of the generations and the many different psychological and spiritual elements of which the human personality is formed. The child receives some of these elements, with the result that his identification with his ancestor is justified. A cycle is built up and completed in this way, the child setting off towards the adult life and old age.

What is the reason for this elaborate and studied setting in which death never has the last word? On the basis of the all too brief outline that I have provided of attitudes among certain ethnic groups in Africa towards death and the hereafter, it is possible to suggest several reasons.

In the first place, it is important to remember that the death of the individual is not ignored in Africa—nothing can be done about it—but that it seems to be powerless in contrast to collective death and life which continues from generation to generation. If this collective life continues, it is not simply because of the number of children that it produces—although children are, of course, its first victory against death—but because it submits to many norms and recognised values to be intangible. These norms and values are themselves also subject to the contingency of this world and are therefore constantly exposed to the risk of being changed. If they change, then the group whose identity they safeguard is also in danger of changing. The rules governing these norms and values have therefore to have a basis elsewhere and it is the function of the ancestors of the group to protect them. The status of ancestor consequently implies 'a certain knowledge and wisdom, . . . a function of supervision, . . . control . . . and judgment'.[20] No member of the group has the right to leave the path pointed out by the ancestors and anyone who does is in grave danger of being recalled sharply to the reality of the situation and of being visited by misfortune.

On the other hand, one of the most important insights in the whole of African thought is that nothing is equal to life itself. Paradoxically, however, if its value is to be recognised, man has to learn the way of death and know that life is revealed in a permanent process of going further. Being initiated into adult life, for example, is an encounter with and an overcoming of death. The frequent exchanges of food between the living and the dead in African communities can be understood in the light of this dynamism of life. The dead feed the living—they are at the source of the fertility of the fields and of women. The living feed the dead with their libations and sacrifices. As M. Fournier has pointed out, 'food points both to our continued existence and to our fragility. It keeps us alive, but at the same time it is also the sign of our death. An offering of food to the dead means that they are still alive and must not be left alone in hunger and thirst, in other words, forgotten and abandoned'.[21]

If there is in fact collective life after death in the hereafter, then every ancestor needs to be remembered and his name has to be invoked when sacrifices are made so that he can survive. What is the fate of those who are remembered by no one and whose name is forgotten? In the Fon language the same word is used for 'to be' and 'to be called'. This is why it is so important for an African to have descendants who will survive him and who will invoke his name from time to time when sacrifices are offered.

Finally, it is only for convenience that Africans speak about life and death as such. They do not live—they are more or less alive. In the same way, they also talk of death in the plural. The moment of death is the visible threshold of a slow process which began a long time previously and which will continue until the time when everything is blotted out from the memory. There are stages in the process of dying—the last breath, the slow dissociation from spiritual principles, the acquisition of a new status by means of the funeral rite, sacrifices offered to the ancestors and then, very gradually, because of the increasing number of generations, entry into anonymity. The Africans refuse to give one meaning to death, just as they do not give one meaning to life, which forms its counterpoint.

It is obvious that, confronted with this concept of the hereafter and this idea of man's relationship with the dead, the Christian message inevitably must have struck Africans as strange. In the past too, our own rural traditions with regard to the dead played a very important part and it was a widely held conviction in Europe that, contrary to the teaching of the Church, 'the dead took a long time to die definitively. They came back or threatened to return for months, even years, to the places and houses where they had lived during this life. It was therefore necessary to come to terms with them, get rid of them without treating them abruptly and make their life outside the grave easy. The Church went on combatting this conviction that those who had died survived more or less temporarily on earth'.[22] An example of this belief that persisted until less than a century ago was the practice of leaving a log burning in the fireplace—because the dead are always cold—and a table full of food—because they need to eat—in houses in many parts of France on the night of the first and second of November, when the dead came back, so it was thought, to haunt their houses.

The African peasants have similar practices today that are just as respectable and everything points to the fact that their ancestors are not yet ready to give up haunting their dreams and that they will have to go on for a long time submitting themselves to their ancestors' will.

Translated by David Smith

Notes

1. See L. V. Thomas *Cinq essais sur la mort négro-africaine* (Dakar 1965); *ibid. Anthropologie de la mort* (Paris 1966). A very useful introductory book is L. V. Thomas and R. Luneau *La terre africaine et ses religions* (Paris 1975), especially 'Les vivants et les morts' pp. 93-106, and 'La mort et les rites funéraires', pp. 246-263.

2. See L. V. Thomas and R. Luneau *Les sages dépossédés* (Paris 1977) pp. 147-156.

3. A. Boulanger *Recherches sur la société et la religion Zela*, Diplôme, Ecole Pratique des Hautes Etudes, Section 5 (1977) p. 175.

4. See R. Luneau *Les chemins de la noce. Le mariage et la femme dans la société rurale au Mali* (Lille 1975) pp. 230-234.

5. This is the case in certain Central African ethnic groups.

6. L. V. Thomas has provided the text of a questioning of the dead of this kind in L. V. Thomas and R. Luneau *Les religions d'Afrique Noire. Textes et Traditions sacrés* (Paris 1969) pp. 233-249.

7. G. Guedou 'La mort chez les Fon, mythe et langage' *Afrique et Langage* 1 (1975) pp. 41-56.

8. P. Saulnier *Noms de naissance, conception du monde et systèmes de valeurs chez les Gun du Bénin* Diplôme de l'E.H.E.S.S. (Paris 1976) p. 167.

9. See G. Guedou *op. cit.* pp. 42-43.

10. F. J. Nicolas 'Les notions d'âme et de divinité en Afrique Occidentale' *Anthropos* (1956) p. 1962.

11. See J. Boulanger *Les âges de la vie chez la femme Tabwa (Zaire)* Institut Catholique de Paris (1977).

12. M. Fournier 'Rituels funéraires Sar' *Afrique et Parole* 37-38 (July 1972) p 24.

13. M. Fournier *op. cit.* p. 12.

14. I have relied here to a great extent on A. Boulanger's study *op. cit.*

15. R. M. Segbenou *Gbeto, Proposition pour une anthropologie africaine* (Lyons 1976) p. 89.

16. R. M. Segbenou *op. cit.* p. 89.

17. R. Bastide 'Religions africaines et structures de civilisation' *Présence Africaine* 66 (1968) p. 103.

18. P. Erny *Sur les sentiers de l'Université. Autobiographies d'étudiants zairois* (Paris 1977) p. 286.

19. See M. C. and E. Ortigues *Oedipe africain* (Paris 1966).

20. See A. Boulanger *op. cit.* p. 212.

21. See M. Fournier *op. cit.* p. 33.

22. J. Delumeau *Le christianisme va-t-il mourir?* (Paris 1977) p. 28.

Jan Nelis

God and Heaven in the
Old Testament

CHRISTIANS have a tendency to confuse God and heaven when they
are speaking—they say, for example, without distinction: 'Heaven only
knows' or 'God knows'. The Jews also did this. We have only to glance
through the second book of Maccabees to see how the author sometimes
speaks of God, the Lord or the Almighty and at others of heaven (2 Macc.
2 : 21; 3 : 20, 34; 7 : 11; 8 : 20; 9 : 5, 20; 14 : 34; 15 : 8, 21, 34). This way
of speaking about God was clearly customary in the Jewish diaspora in
Egypt. There are also several examples in the Greek translation of the
Old Testament, the Septuagint, of the word 'heaven' being used where
the original Hebrew text had 'God' (Job 22 : 26; Ps. 7 : 10; 90 : 1; Isa.
14 : 13; 38 : 14). The name of God never occurs in 1 Maccabees, not even
when the author is quoting from the Old Testament. In every case the
word 'heaven' is used (1 Macc. 3 : 18, 19, 50, 60; 4 : 10, 24, 40, 55;
12 : 15; 16 : 3). This usage is evidence both of the awe felt by Jews with
regard to the holy name of God and of the close association between
heaven and God.

In the light of our knowledge of comparative religion, we recognise that
this association between heaven and the deity points to the fact that, like
Zeus, Jupiter, Varuna, Anu and so on, the God of the Bible was the
concrete form assumed by the exalted, incorruptible, powerful and transcendent ideas that occurred to man as *homo religiosus* when he con-
templated heaven. The Old Testament image of God may therefore have
a uranic character and be based on man's intuition of heaven as the
symbol and embodiment of what is sacred and absolute. As such, then, it
differs on the one hand from the image of the deity that was expressed in

22

the gods of the underworld, the water and the earth and, on the other, from that of the gods of fertility, the moon and the sun.

Is this association between God and heaven found in all the parts of the Old Testament, even the earliest? If it is, then we clearly have a theological constant which might form the Old Testament background to the idea of 'Our Father in heaven'. In this article, I shall examine the relationship between God and heaven and come to a number of conclusions.

1. THE USE AND MEANING OF THE WORD 'HEAVEN'

What did the Israelite mean by the word 'heaven' when he made a connection between it and the word 'God'? 'Heaven' (Hebrew: *šāmayîm*, Aramaic: *šᵉmayyā*) occurs 458 times in the Masoretic text and about 667 times, taking into account the textual variants, in the Septuagint, including the deuterocanonical books. In the protocanonical books of the Septuagint, the word 'heaven' occurs 498 times—this is forty times more than in the Hebrew text. In fact, there are fifty-four places in the Septuagint where the word 'heaven' occurs without any corresponding use in the Hebrew text. There are also fourteen places where the word occurs in the Hebrew text, but not in the corresponding Greek text.

Taking into account the context in which the word 'heaven' occurs, several different categories of use can be distinguished. Quite often—about 180 times—it is used together with 'earth', sometimes as the corresponding term in a parallelism and very frequently as one of the two closely associated words 'heaven and earth'. Used in this sense, 'heaven' forms part of a description of the universe that is familiar to us today. It is the part of the world in which we live, which is not removed from our grasp, but on which we and our earth also depend.

The second category includes the many Old Testament texts where 'heaven' is used in an astronomical context. In these texts, we read of the sun, the moon and the stars 'in heaven'. I would also include in this category the various meteorological phenomena that are mentioned in the Old Testament in the context of 'heaven': the clouds, the rain, snow and hail, the fire from heaven and so on.

A third category includes the 'birds of heaven'. This phrase occurs forty-two times in the Old Testament. Although it may strike us as strange, this is not an exclusively biblical way of speaking. The birds are also described as inhabiting heaven in the Ugaritic and Akkadian texts. It has sometimes been suggested that the Hebrew word *šāmayîm* also meant the 'air', because birds move through the air. Biblical Hebrew had no word for 'air' and later Hebrew filled in this gap by using the Greek word *aer*, pronounced *awir*. It would seem that the Jews were not conscious of the lack of a word for 'air' until the second or first century B.C. This would also appear to indicate that they believed that the space immediately above the earth had its own being, distinct from that of heaven, a being characterised by the presence of winds and by differences in temperature.

A similar development has also taken place in our own languages. 'Air' and 'heaven' were originally synonyms for the space, vault or roof above the earth. This is obvious in such phrases as 'there is rain in the air' on the one hand and 'the birds flying in the air' on the other. The first example differs from the second in that there is no sense of crossing a barrier in the second, in which we think of the air as part of our own environment. In the case of a 'tower rising up high into the air' too, we remain firmly in our own sphere. This is obvious if we think of the Tower of Babel with its top not 'in heaven' (Gen. 11 : 4), but 'in the air'. Most modern readers would find such a translation of the text trivial, so that even a modern translation such as that of the Jerusalem Bible has 'a tower with its top reaching heaven'. The biblical concept is covered by our word 'air' only in the sense of the space high above us in which not only the clouds, but also the heavenly bodies move. Unlike the 'beasts of the field' and the 'fish of the sea', the birds have access to this part of the world. If man, however, tries to reach that space by building a tower, that is, for the biblical author, an act of hybris and a form of rebellion against the God who gave man the earth as the place where he should live and work.

A fourth category consists of those texts in which the word *šāmayîm* has to some extent an architectural significance or secondary meaning. It occurs nine times in Gen. 1 with the meaning of firmament. The Hebrew word *rāqîaᶜ* in this context certainly means a hard, firm covering, trodden flat like earth, in other words, the firmament, which has to bear a mass of water (see, for example, Ps. 148 : 4) that can be made to fall down through sluices (Gen. 7 : 11; 2 Kings 7 : 2, 9; Mal. 3 : 10).

This clearly points to a theory about the structure of the world that is as primitive as the poetical idea of the heavenly tent that also occurs in the Bible (see Ps. 104 : 2; Isa. 40 : 22). This second image, in which heaven is compared with a tent, should not, however, be understood cosmologically. The underlying intention is quite different—heaven protects the earth and man who lives there as a tent protects those within it against evil influences from outside. It is quite likely that heaven in Ps. 104 : 2 is intended to represent Yahweh's tent and that the meteorological phenomena mentioned subsequently should be understood as serving him.

The protective function of heaven as a firmament is also clear from the texts in which this image occurs. In Job 37 : 18, its hardness is compared with that of a metal mirror. In 2 Sam. 22 : 8, the foundations and, in Job 26 : 11, the pillars supporting heaven point to the firmness of the covering. What is indicated in these texts is the protection given by the firmament to the cosmos against the destructive power of the primeval waters.

In a fifth category of texts, *šāmayîm* is the dwelling place of God. Various images are used to indicate this concept in the Old Testament. The most striking of these is that of the stronghold (Ps. 78 : 26; 150 : 1). The bulwark set up by Yahweh against his enemies (Ps. 8 : 3) is also presumably heaven. Heaven, then, is also the symbol of God's inaccessibility.

2. AN ANALYSIS OF SEVERAL TEXTS

Two texts—Exod. 24 : 10 and Ezek. 1 : 22—have a special place in this fifth category. According to Exod. 24 : 9-11, Moses, Aaron, Nadab and Abihu went up Mount Sinai to witness a theophany. Although the text says that 'they saw the God of Israel', no attempt at all is made to describe his form. Unlike Isa. 6 : 1, the text does not even refer to a throne and it would appear that the author believed that it would be contrary to the idea of God's transcendence to suggest that he was sitting on a throne like a human king. Attention is drawn rather to what was 'under his feet'. This is presumably the little bench on which the royal person on the throne placed his feet. It was also a sign of power. There are representations of Egyptian and Mesopotamian kings with their feet resting on the necks of their enemies, an image that also occurs in Ps. 110 : 1 (see also 2 Sam. 22 : 39; 1 Kings 5 : 17; Ps. 18 : 39; 47 : 4). The same image is also used in Ps. 8 : 7, where the psalmist wishes to show the power of man's rule over creation.

What, then, is under God's feet in Exod. 24 : 10? It is something that does not form part of the ordinary world of human experience and is therefore compared with a 'handiwork' well known to man. The use of this word indicates that the author was not thinking of a natural object, but of something made by man, though precisely what he had in mind cannot be deduced with certainty from the Hebrew text. One reason for this uncertainty is that it is difficult to know precisely what the Hebrew word *sappîr* means, although we can say that it was undoubtedly a precious or semi-precious stone set into the handiwork and that it was probably lapis lazuli or lazulite. Another reason for uncertainty is the word in the Hebrew text that is associated with *sappîr*; *libhᵉnath*, in the phrase *libhᵉnath hassappîr*. Following the Greek translation of the Septuagint, *libhᵉnath* was connected with the word *lᵉbhēnah*, a brick or tile, and it was concluded that the text meant 'a tiled floor (pavement) of lapis lazuli'.

The word *libhᵉnath*, however, also means—with a vowel change—

'whiteness' (the stem *lābhan* means 'white'). In that case, the text would indicate the whiteness of the stone or its brilliance. The purity or brilliance of precious stones is also mentioned in several Ugaritic texts, where the same word as that used in the second part of the Hebrew phrase in Exod. 24 : 10 (*sappîr*) occurs: 'the whiteness of *sappîr*, as clear as heaven itself'. What is obvious, then, is that the biblical author was more concerned with the brilliance and purity of the stone than with its colour. It is also clear that he was aware of a close connection between the 'handiwork' under God's feet and heaven. In his view, heaven—radiant, sometimes azure and at others sharply white—was the footstool of the creator.

The word *sappîr* also occurs in Ezek. 1, where it refers to God's throne (Ezek. 1 : 26; see also 10 : 1). This throne is placed on a kind of firmament that is compared with rock-crystal (Ezek. 1 : 22). In the Hebrew text, the word for 'ice' is used, but there can be no doubt that this term, like the Greek *krustallos* in the Septuagint, indicates the colourless purity associated with crystalline quartz. Even Pliny thought that rock-crystal was a kind of ice that had become frozen so hard that it could not be thawed. (See his *Naturalis Historia*, Liber XXXVII, 23.) This semi-precious stone had been used as an ornament from the Bronze Age onwards. The prophet Ezekiel was convinced that only something very rare and precious could give any idea of God's exalted existence. It is also clear that he was speaking of heaven when he referred to this firmament on which God's throne stood. The word 'firmament' (*rāqîaᶜ*) always means 'heaven' in all the other places where it occurs in the Old Testament.

Insofar as these texts are descriptive, they have a symbolic character. They do not place God in heaven as though he dwelt there in a palace built above the firmament. The point to things that man knew from his own experience and their aim was to suggest God's transcendence. If, for example, the biblical author describes God's feet resting on heaven, the reader knows that heaven and earth are at the feet of the Creator and are totally dependent on His will.

In Ps. 104 : 3, there would seem to be a heavenly palace in or above the waters of the ocean of heaven. The translation of the French Jerusalem Bible reads: 'You build your upper rooms on the waters'. We have to look at the immediate context for a true interpretation of this part of the verse. Verses 1b-4 refer to the relationship between His creation and Yahweh himself and light (verse 2a), heaven and the waters (2b and 3a), the clouds, the winds and the lightning (3a-4) are all mentioned. The light is called God's garment (2a), the clouds are His chariot and the winds and the flashes of lightning are His messengers and servants (4). Yahweh is said to 'stretch out heaven as a tent' (cf. Isa. 40 : 22) and the author is clearly thinking here of a dwelling place for God himself. This is confirmed by the parallel in the following verse (3a): 'You build *your* upper rooms on the waters'. The concept of the 'upper rooms' indicates a distance from the bustle in the streets of the city—anyone who wants to be alone and undisturbed withdraws into an upper room and closes them off (see Judges 3 : 20 ff; 2 Sam. 19 :1; 1 Kings 17 : 19 ff, etc.). It is clear from the fact that the reference to God's upper rooms is in parallel with the reference to his stretching out heaven like a tent that the author was not thinking here of a retreat somewhere above the firmament. There are two different images, each illustrating in its own way how God is present in his creation. He lives in the radiance of heaven as in a tent that lets some of His glory shine outside through the canvas. The dark water is compared with an upper chamber protecting his glory from the earth.

In my opinion, then, the Hebrew text does not speak of upper rooms built on the water and it would be quite wrong to think that the author is telling us that God built rooms on piles in or on the ocean of heaven. The Hebrew word from which 'upper rooms' is derived may have this meaning, but it is usually synonymous with 'building'. According to the text, God built upper rooms in the water. The meaning of this statement is clear from its context—just as heaven is His tent and the light is His garment, so too is the water His private room. It is obvious that the author would think in this case of the water above the earth.

Another text that should be taken into account in this context is Amos 9 : 6: 'He has built His high dwelling places in the heavens' (translation of the Jerusalem Bible, with a footnote indicating that the word 'steps' occurs in the Hebrew Bible). The Dutch Catholic Willibrord translation interprets these 'steps' in the Hebrew text as *pars pro toto* and has the following version: 'He who builds His exalted throne in heaven'. There are references elsewhere in the Old Testament (1 Kings 10: 19 f; 2 Chron. 9 : 18 f; Isa. 6 : 1) to raised thrones with steps. According to Ps. 103 : 19, Yahweh set up His throne in heaven (see also Ps. 47: 6, 9; 97 : 2). According to Isa. 66 : 1, heaven is His throne and the earth is His footstool.

Precisely what Yahweh built on or above the earth in Amos 9 : 6b is not clear. Most translations, including that of the Jerusalem Bible, speak of 'His vault' and the commonest version is: 'He founded His vault on the earth'. Vaulted buildings were not unknown in Palestine during the age of the kings, but the were presumably little used. It would therefore not be usual to compare the firmament with a vault. What is more, it would be difficult to see in the small, dark vaults that may have existed at that time an image of the wide, light firmament. Finally, there is no suitable philological foundation for the translation 'vault' for the Hebrew *'a gud-dah*, which means a bunch or band. It might be possible to think of 'His troop' of heavenly bodies forming His army and of Yahweh giving these a fixed place above the earth.

It should be clear from my analysis of these texts that the biblical authors expressed God's presence in creation in certain images—His being enthroned above the heavens, His dwelling in the waters, His moving on the wings of the wind and so on—in which they gave form and content to their faith in His exalted state as Creator above His creation and also in His power as ruler.

3. THE ANTIQUITY OF THIS CONCEPT OF GOD

It was during the Persian period that it became customary in Jewish writing to give Yahweh the title of the 'God of heaven'. This title is found, for example, in texts referring to the relationships between Jerusalem and the Achaemenids. The God of the Jews was called the 'God of heaven' by the Persian chancellery (see 2 Chron. 36 : 23; Ezra 1 : 2; 5 : 12; 6 : 9 f; 7 : 12, 21, 23; Neh. 2 : 20). In their letters to the Persian magistrates, the Jews living on Elephantine also called their God the 'God of heaven'.[1] The same title was also used by these Jews in letters to others who shared their faith.[2] Nehemiah himself addressed Yahweh in personal prayer as the 'God of heaven' (Neh. 1 : 4, 5; 2 : 5). The title also occurs in the book of Daniel (Dan. 2 : 18, 19, 37, 44). Jonah told the crew of the ship in which he sailed to Tarshish that he worshipped 'Yahweh, the God of heaven' (Jonah 1 : 9). Other texts in which the 'God of heaven' occurs are Ps. 136 : 26; Tob. 8 : 15; Judith 5 : 8; 6 : 19; 11 : 17.

The only text dating back to the period of Israel's kings which includes this title is Gen. 24 : 7, which is uncertain from the point of view of textual criticism. According to verse 3, Abraham asks his servant to swear an oath by Yahweh 'the God of heaven and the God of earth'. This detailed description is repeated in the Septuagint in verse 7, although the title 'God of heaven' is not present in a Hebrew manuscript. Even if the description of Yahweh as the 'God of heaven' in verse 3 is original, this does not mean that the title has the special significance and emotive force in this context that it has as an official title for Yahweh in the Persian period. In Gen. 24 : 3, it would appear to be an abbreviated description of the sphere of Yahweh's power and rule. It is in any case clear that the people of Israel already regarded Yahweh as a universal God who was also the Lord of heaven. This is why he is called 'God on high' in Mic. 6 : 6. 'On high' here is a translation of the Hebrew *mārôm*, which is synonymous with *šāmayîm*, 'heaven'.

In 1 Kings 20 : 23, 28, the Aramaeans call Yahweh a 'god of the mountains' and there is certainly a close connection in the Old Testament between Yahweh and the holy mountain, the mountain of God, Sinai or Horeb. This was, of course, the mountain to which Elijah went (1 Kings 19) and encountered God. This encounter is described as being accompanied by an earthquake and atmospheric phenomena such as thunder and lightning. These phenomena point to the 'heavenly' nature of the deity who reveals Himself to Elijah on Horeb. The theophany on Mount Sinai (Exod. 19: 16) also took place to the accompaniment of peals of thunder and flashes of lightning and dark clouds covered the mountain. The theology and the style of the Elohist is discernible in this description. The Yahwist's outline (Exod. 19: 18) is different: 'And Mount Sinai was wrapped in smoke because Yahweh descended upon it in fire; and the smoke of it went up like the smoke of a kiln'.

The important word in this text is 'descended': Yahweh had come down on to Mount Sinai. According to the Yahwist, then, God was not a 'god of the mountains' who had His palace on the summit of Sinai. On the contrary, he was a God who was raised far above Sinai. This 'coming down' is stressed repeatedly in the book of Exodus (3: 8; 19: 11, 20; 34: 5) and it even occurs in the early story of the Tower of Babel (Gen. 11: 5 ff) and in Jacob's dream of the ladder which reached from earth to heaven so that God's angels could go up and come down. (Gen. 28: 12). Yahweh is also praised in many of the earliest hymns that are preserved in the Bible as a God who comes from heaven to help His people, whose army consists of the stars and who spreads panic among Israel's enemies with His rain and hail, thunder and lightning (see Deut. 33: 26 ff; Judges 5: 4, 20; 2 Sam. 22).

4. HEAVEN AND MAN'S HAPPINESS

Man's happiness is closely linked in the Old Testament with the fertility of the earth. A constantly recurring theme is that this fertility is a gift from heaven and that it ultimately goes back to God himself. When, for example, at the time of Elijah, Yahweh closed heaven so that a drought occurred. The people starved (1 Kings 17). Hosea, on the other hand, predicted happiness for Israel on her return to Yahweh as her bride-groom: 'I will answer the heavens and they shall answer the earth; the earth shall answer the grain, the wine and the oil' (Hos. 2: 21 f; 'answer' here meaning 'favourable to'). The Second Isaiah also expresses the same longing for the happiness that comes from heaven: 'Showers, heavens, from above, and let the skies rain down righteousness; let the earth open, that abundance may sprout forth and let it cause prosperity to spring up' (Isa. 45: 8).

The words 'abundance' and 'prosperity' are replaced in many trans-lations by 'salvation' and 'righteousness', to provide a more spiritual interpretation of the text. In any case, it is clear here that the mythical view of heaven and earth underlies the passage, heaven pouring out its seed into the lap of mother earth, so that she can give life to a luxuriant growth of the plants that feed men and animals. In the light of Israel's return to Palestine, the prophet would clearly have been thinking primarily of the paradise-like state of that country. Repatriation is the salvation to which the people had to look forward. At the same time, however, God's purified people would also be made happy by His justice.

The rhythm of human life is also determined, according to the Old Testament, by heaven (see Ps. 104 : 19-23; Neh. 4 : 21). The sun and moon regulate the months, the seasons and the feasts (Gen. 1 : 14-18; Ps. 104 : 19 f; 136 : 8 f). In Job 38 : 33, we read of the 'ordinances of the heavens' imposing 'their rule on the earth'. The Israelites believed that the harmonious order that was manifested in heaven and its phenomena was lasting and unchangeable (see, for example, Ps. 89 : 3; 119 : 89) and that it was therefore able to guarantee man's happiness. An even more certain guarantee was provided by God's justice. According to Isa. 51 : 6, 'even though heaven vanishes like smoke . . . my salvation will be for ever'. (The translation that frequently appears: 'heaven—or the heavens—will vanish like smoke . . . but my salvation will be for ever' is not correct.)

In more recent Old Testament texts, faith in the stability of the contemporary world order seems to be much weaker. There are, for example, many impressive images in these later texts which provide a poetical interpretation of God's intervention, either to punish or to save man. (See Isa. 13 : 13; 50 : 3; Joel 2 : 10; 4 : 15; Amos 8 : 9; Hab. 3 : 11 etc.) In Isa. 34 : 4, on the other hand, there would seem to be a proclamation of the end of heaven: 'The armies of heaven rot. The heavens are rolled up like a scroll and their armies all drop like leaves, like vine leaves falling' (Jerusalem Bible translation). The withering and falling of leaves can also be applied to heavenly bodies that lose their lustre and is found, for example, in Ezek. 32 : 7 and Joel 2 : 10, where the stars are also said to 'become dark'. The Hebrew word means to waste or rot away and this refers to the weakening of the stars' light.

The rolling up of heaven has been wrongly interpreted as a rolling up of the vault of heaven, with an idea similar to that in 2 Pet. 3 : 10 or the Sybilline Oracles 3 : 80 ff in mind. In fact, however, the author was thinking of the dark clouds unrolling like a scroll over the earth and obscuring the light of the sun, moon and stars. The same meteorological phenomenon is used in Isa. 50 : 3, where the author speaks of the mourning or sack-cloth covering heaven.

What is the meaning of the 'new heaven and the new earth' that will be created by God according to Isa. 65 : 17 and 66 : 22? Is the idea of creating something new justified if the present world is not consumed by fire or by some other disaster? It is certainly justified, because the term 'create' is not confined in the Old Testament to the sense of bringing something in its totality into being without the previous existence of matter. Re-creation or renewal is a frequently occurring concept in the Old Testament. According to Ps. 51 : 10, for example, God will 'create' a clean heart and 'renew' a steadfast spirit. Creation and renewal are parallel in this verse and they refer to two factors: clean and steadfast. God, in other words, re-creates and renews man's sinful heart and wavering spirit and makes him clean and steadfast.

The words 'create' and 'new' are used in this sense in Isa. 65 : 17 and 66 : 22. The way in which this new creation is made manifest is clear from the context of the first text: life will be a paradise on earth, as in Isa. 11 : 6 ff. The description of the new Jerusalem in Isa. 54 : 11 ff should also be understood in the same way, in other words, as a description of the eschatological re-creation of life on this earth. Despite the references to precious stones such as jasper, lazulite, agate and carbuncles in the rebuilding of the city, the Second Isaiah was not describing a heavenly fortress like that described, for example, in Gal. 4 : 26; Rev. 21 : 10; Heb. 12 : 22; 13 : 14. On the contrary, he was speaking of the holy city to which the exiled Israelites would be taken back from Babylon by God, their shepherd. The Israelites were comforted by God's promise that He would rebuild the destroyed city and make it into a stronghold of peace.

Is the idea that those who have been justified are received into heaven when they die expressed in the Old Testament? It should be clear from what I have already said in this article that the Israelites had considerable difficulties with the concept of heaven and God's presence in it. There is no doubt that the idea of Yahweh's court in heaven (see, for example, 1 Kings 22 : 19 ff; Job 1 : 6 ff; 2 : 1 ff; Ps. 89 : 6 ff; Dan. 7 : 10; Tob. 12 : 15) was familiar to the Israelites, but, at least according to the evidence in the Old Testament, man had no place in that court. Man was made in the image of God (Gen. 1 : 26 ff; 9 : 6; Ps. 8 : 6 ff; Ecclus. 17 : 3; Wis. 2 : 23), but the Israelites did not believe, as Plato did, that the human soul was imprisoned in the dungeon of the body. It is clear from Gen. 2 : 7, that they believed that man had been fashioned by God from the earth and that God had breathed the breath of life into him. Such a being could, in their view, not find a place in heaven.

There are, however, two persons in particular who are said in the Old Testament to have been taken up into the heavenly sphere. These are Enoch and Elijah. The reference to Enoch's reception into heaven is very concise, both in Gen. 5 : 24 and in Ecclus. 44 : 16. It is not said that he died (see Heb. 11 : 5), but that he 'walked' with God, in other words, that he associated with God on terms of familiarity. This aspect of Enoch's existence is repeated in Gen. 5 : 22 and 24 and, in the second case, is linked with his 'disappearance'. This disappearance has been theologically interpreted as a taking or reception by God. Where he was taken is not said. The Hebrew word *lāqah*, to take, receive, presumably had a technical meaning in this context. The same root is used in the Epic of Gilgamesh, XI, 196 to describe the disappearance of the hero of the deluge, Utnapishtim the 'Faraway'. Until the deluge occurred. Utnapishtim was an ordinary mortal, but afterwards he was equal to the gods: 'They took me and made me reside far away, at the mouth of the rivers'.

The same verb, *lāqah*, is also used in the account of Elijah's ascension (2 Kings 2 : 3, 5), where it is explained, however, in the following way: 'When Yahweh was about to take Elijah up to heaven by a whirlwind' (2 Kings 2 : 1). The same description is also found in verse 11, where there is also a reference to fire. This fire, in the form of a chariot drawn by horses, takes Elijah up to heaven. (See also Ecclus. 48 : 9.) If the Old Testament idea of God's court in heaven is borne in mind, the only possible interpretation of this 'taking up' into heaven is that the Israelites believed that the prophet was given a place among the beings surrounding God. For the Israelites, this was undoubtedly an exceptional privilege and it is interesting in this context to note the scorn with which Isaiah spoke of the aspirations of those who wanted to 'climb up' to heaven (Isa. 14 : 13 ff). The idea that Elijah was taken up into heaven while he was still alive (2 Kings 2 :1 ff) is linked with the conviction that he would return to earth at the end of time (Mal. 3 : 23).

There are also references in Ps. 49 : 15 and 73 : 24 to being 'taken up' or 'received' in a context which is reminiscent of Enoch's being taken up in Gen. 5 : 24. Death is represented in these texts as a descent into the kingdom of the dead and God's 'taking up' is contrasted with this. The psalmist certainly did not mean by this 'taking up' that God was protecting him from an early death. If this was his intention, he too would in the end have died like the sinners and his psalm would have been meaningless. The text can only be meaningful if it expresses the psalmist's expectation that he would be taken up by God from the earth so that he would be with God, whereas the sinners would go down into the realm of the dead. In Ps. 73 : 24, this being taken up is associated with God's glory and therefore clearly points to man's continued existence in God's world. Ps. 73 : 25 also contains a striking testimony to deep insight into the nature of human happiness, which is to be found not in heaven, as the dwelling place of the immortals, or on earth, as the world of man, but in union with God, man's rock for ever.

A new stage in Israel's thinking about man's fate and heaven can be found in the fairly late book of Wisdom, the author of which was obviously influenced by Hellenistic ideas about man, especially in the emphasis that he places on the soul rather than the body as the centre of man's being (see, for example, Wis. 8 : 19 ff). For this reason, he is able to speak about the fate of the just when they die and in particular immediately after their death, when they are waiting for definitive recompense or retribution at the last judgment (3 : 7 ff). Their existence is described by the word 'peace' and this peace comes from their union with the Lord (3 : 1-3; 5 : 15 ff). They have an assurance of immortality because they have kept God's law (6 : 18 ff).

The theme of paradise plays an important part in Old Testament thinking about man's happiness. Paradise is the golden age in the beginning. Men hope for the return of that age and its return is prophesied. Both the original paradise and the messianic paradise, however, are on earth and form part of man's world. The first people were happy in paradise and the same happiness will be known by the last generation of mankind, but in between these two extremities man lives in an age of harsh suffering. Timeless happiness is only possible for those whom God, in his mercy, takes out of this world. According to many of the later writings that were not included in the canon of the Old Testament, paradise still exists either somewhere far away or else even in heaven. Heaven has a distinctly eschatological aspect in these writings and in such New Testament texts as Heb. 11 : 13 ff; 13 : 14, man is even called a 'stranger and exile' on earth and a citizen of heaven. (See also Eph. 2 : 19.)

Translated by David Smith

Notes

1. See A. Cowley *Aramic Papyri of the Fifth Century B.C.* (Oxford 1923) No. 30, 2 : 27; 31 : 2; 32 : 3.
2. *ibid.* No 38, 3 : 5; 40 : 1.

Aelred Cody

The New Testament

IN THE books of the New Testament, just as in those of the Old, the word 'heaven' refers primarily, of course, to the sky above us, which the ancients thought of as a dome, or occasionally as a tent, serving as a firmament to which the stars were attached, with the pair 'heaven and earth' or the triad 'heaven, earth and sea' representing the entire created universe. That primary material sense of the word need not occupy us here. The abandonment today of speculative constructions like those involving several superimposed heavens, based on a view of the material universe itself which is no longer held by either astronomers or by philosophers, is no loss to theology, even though such constructions were used at times in passing apocalyptic allusions to paradise, as in 2 Cor. 12: 2-4. But when heaven is a symbol of a reality transcending our sensory experience, difficult for human minds to comprehend and for human language to express, the symbolic language needs to be pondered anew in every generation, and the reality understood. Our task here is that of reviewing concepts involving heaven in a more symbolic way in the New Testament itself and in the world of ideas in which the New Testament authors moved.

1. ESCHATOLOGICAL HEAVEN IN THE JEWISH WORLD

Theological reflection on heaven is grounded on the idea of heaven as the place where God is and where mortal man is not. This originally spatial image, used in the mythic language of ancient Oriental civilisations, adopted in Israel, and found in the Hellenic world's eventual identification of Olympus with the heaven above, perdures in New Testament times, although those with a more philosophical bent of mind in Israel and elsewhere had seen clearly already that God can not be encompassed by limits of space anywhere in the universe. In the last centuries of the pre-Christian era and on into New Testament times Old Testament concepts of heaven were supplemented by the visions of religious Jewish apocalyptic writers, disillusioned with this earthly world, looked upon as godless and evil, and longing for a better one in which the pious would enjoy a new existence in a world somehow heavenly, with God. The older, classical, Jewish eschatology, with its expectations of a great future day in which the familiar Jewish institutions of this world would enter a new and better period, began to be complemented by a new and more universal eschatology, itself not without roots in certain prophetic writings, in which all the just would achieve a happier existence in a radically different world of a future age which would replace the present unhappy one after a final moment of judgment and destruction. This led to speculation about two ages: the present one and its future replacement. The future age was to be the age of salvation from the misery of the present one, but questions having to do with who were to be saved from punishment, where they were to be in the coming age, and the kind of existence they were to lead there received various visionary answers from various apocalyptic authors. In general, the answers depended on an author's view of the beneficiaries of salvation. The majority held salvation to be for Israel as a whole, or for the righteous within the Jewish community (an idea implicit in Dn. 12 : 1-4 and echoed in Lk 19 : 9), but occasionally Jewish writers of the intertestamental period saw salvation in the coming age as something to be hoped for by righteous men of all nations, on condition of some kind of association with Israel or, in certain passages in the Apocalypses of Esdras and Baruch (both quite late) and in book III of the Sibylline Oracles, for all men serving God rightly even without any association with Israel.

In Jewish writings of this period the idea of eschatological victory for the righteous in a future age on *earth* continued to predominate. This is somewhat true of the sectaries represented at Qumran, although some documents from Qumran do show expectations of a common lot of the elect of Israel with angelic or heavenly beings (1 QH 3 : 21-23; 6 : 13; 11 : 11-13; 1 QM 10 : 10-12) and the *Rule of the Community* speaks of the elect of mankind standing before God forever (1 QS 11 : 16-17), while one passage in the Qumran War Scroll explicitly associates the victorious elect of God's people with the armies of angels in heaven with God (1 QM 12 : 1-5). The holy city of Jerusalem and the land promised to Abraham, transformed, fitted eschatological existence of which the beneficiaries would be Jews or pagans assimilated to Jews, but they were less adequate as places for the enjoyment of some kind of salvation by all the just without ethnic distinction. It is especially in passages by Jewish authors with this less exclusively ethnic view of the coming age that heaven itself began to be represented as the place for the just, as in Henoch 104 : 2-6, in which the gates of heaven at the end of this age are seen opening to the just, who will be associates of the angels. Less explicit in visual description but more expressive of the real sense of heavenly beatitude is what we find somewhat later, in the authentically Jewish sections of the Apocalypse of Esdras (4 Ezra or 2 Esdras). There it is said that the righteous will see the glory of Him who takes them up (7 : 91), hastening to see the face of Him whom they served in life (7 : 98), after this present world has come to an end.

2. ESCHATOLOGICAL HEAVEN IN THE NEW TESTAMENT

In Christianity the concept of heaven as the 'place' for the enjoyment of eschatological goods became general. The Messianic kingdom became the kingdom of the heavens (in Matthew) or the heavenly kingdom (2 Tm. 4 : 18), where our proper commonwealth is (Phil. 3 : 20). Our reward is in heaven (Mt 5 : 12; Lk 6 : 23), and it is there that we are to store up treasures which are not subject to the losses to which the treasures of this world are exposed (Mt 6 : 20; Lk 12 : 33). Our earthly dwelling or body will be taken away, but it will be replaced by an eternal one in heaven (2 Cor. 5 : 1-10). Christians should rejoice in fact, because their names are no longer written on the census lists of an earthly realm but on those of a heavenly one (Lk 10 : 20).

The basic reason for this development lies simply in the realisation that the greatest of all joys consists in being delivered entirely from the tirbulations of this world and living forever with God, and that this is now possible for mankind because of Christ's saving work. Since Jesus himself rose from the dead and was glorified by ascending into heaven, the apostle, working that the elect might achieve salvation, expressed that salvation in terms of similarity to what Christ himself has done: if we die with Him, we shall also live with Him, and if we endure, we shall also reign with Him (2 Tm. 2 : 8, 10-12). For St. John, Christ will draw all unto Himself when He has been lifted up (Jn. 12 : 32), for He is the way (14 : 6). He is also the pioneer (archēgos) of salvation (Hb 2 : 10) or of life (Ac 3 : 15) because God exalted him as pioneer and saviour to his right hand (Ac 5 : 31). The author of the Epistle to the Hebrews presents the life of Christians on earth as a journey towards their heavenly home and resting place (Hb 3 : 7-4; 11), with the way opened by Christ (4 : 14; 6 : 20; 8 : 1-2; 9 : 15; 10 : 12, 19-22).

In texts like these the characteristic Jewish doctrine of the two ages remains implicit, but the eschatological future age has been transformed, with all Christian life tending ultimately not towards a final age exclusively, in a transformed world (the idea remains in 2 Pt. 3 : 10-13; Apoc.

21 : 1, which speak of a new, transformed, cosmic heaven and earth), but towards heaven, in the wake of Christ. Heaven is not the material, spatial heaven set above the earth with which it forms a part of the created universe. It is rather the antithesis of the created, visible heaven and earth, and the symbolic expression of a transcendent mode of existence characterised by divine glory.

The background to this sublimated concept of heaven has been sought in various quarters of antiquity. A certain amount of dualism is obviously involved, but the dualistic concepts themselves are of varied provenance. Underlying the properly Jewish concept of the two ages, present and future, one may sense the influence of an Iranian type of dualistic thought about good and evil principles, for the present age was looked upon largely as one subject to the forces of evil, whether worldly or demonic, while the future age would be fully subject to God. For that matter, even the idea of some kind of heavenly existence for the immortal, found in different forms among Pythagoreans, certain Neo-Platonists, and eventually Gnostics and adherents of the mystery religions, has distant Indo-Iranian antecedents as well as Egyptian ones. But more important for the sublimated concept of heaven as the ideal sphere for a salvation consisting of liberation from the limitations of earthly existence is a dualism of Platonic stamp characteristic of the Hellenistic world. In dualistic thinking of this sort the heavenly world is the ideal world of perfect, eternal realities, of which earthly phenomena are but imperfect, transitory shadows. Derived from this was the concept of the superiority of what is perceived by the spiritual faculties of mind or intellect to what is perceived by the senses: the sense-perceptible world is earthly, but the world perceived by the spiritual faculties is heavenly. Occasionally the originally Stoic ideal of freedom from the corporeal seems to have made itself felt among cultivated Jews and among early Christian thinkers as well.

3. HEAVENLY LIFE IN PRESENT AND FUTURE

The idea of a heavenly mode of existence in the future, when life in the present age has come to a close, was relatively easy to integrate with an eschatology of the two ages, as long as the final age was looked upon as being entirely in the future. But in the Christian proclamation of salvation and new life, the future age, although still future, has already begun with Christ's saving acts. In some Jewish apocalypses the just are seen in a new paradise in heaven after the end of the present world (Slavic Henoch 65 : 9; Apocalypse of Baruch 51 : 10-11; Testament of the Twelve Patriarchs: Test. of Daniel 5), but Jesus, without mentioning heaven explicitly, tells the good thief crucified beside Him that on that same day they will be together in paradise (Lk. 23 : 43). The kingdom of God (which in Matthew is also 'the kingdom of the heavens') has already arrived with Christ (Mt. 12 : 28; Lk. 17 : 20-21), and yet its coming is still awaited (Mt. 16 : 20). St. Paul speaks in different places of a present salvation or of a future salvation. In Rm. 8 : 10-12 he says that if Christ is in us 'the body is dead because of sin, while the pneuma or spirit *is* life because of righteousness (see also Ga. 2 : 20; Col. 3 : 3-4), and yet he goes on to say that 'He who raised Christ Jesus from the dead *will* also vivify your dead bodies through the spirit dwelling in you'. The idea of a specifically heavenly mode of existence in which we share already on earth is not explicit in the Pauline letters, however; according to Phil. 3 : 20 our commonwealth is in heaven, but the idea expressed there is that, unlike those who are occupied with earthly thoughts (3 : 19), our thoughts and concerns are turned towards heaven, with a mind to the future. In the Fourth Gospel, with its accentuated reflection on the heavenly origin of Christ (Jn. 3 : 13, 31; 6 : 38, 41-42, 51) the bread which He gives to His followers already in this world is from heaven, for it is Himself (6 : 32-33, 41, 50-51, 58), and though Christians are not said to share in 'heavenly' life we do read in the Fourth Gospel that he who believes (3 : 36; 6 : 47), or he who eats the flesh and drinks the blood of Christ (6 : 54), has eternal life, which, in the Hellenistic thought put to work in this gospel, amounts practically to the same thing. A condition for being brought to glory with the exalted Christ is that already in this life we be not of this world (7 : 33-35; 8 : 22-23).

The author of the Epistle to the Hebrews is unique among New Testament writers in employing the Platonising concept of two worlds, the eternal, heavenly one and the transient, earthly one, in such a way that the realities of the heavenly one are already available to Christians in this world. As a result, in a number of passages in Hebrews we find the apocalyptic age of future eschatological benefits transposed into a celestial, eternal age of salvation which already has its effects for Christians still living in this world. The two ages are *already* made (Hb. 1 : 2; 11 : 3) and are completed with the appearance of Christ (9 : 26). We are still pilgrims on the way to the heavenly city (13 : 14), and yet we have already arrived there and are enjoying a fellowship with Christ and with the angels and saints (12 : 22). In 10 : 1 we read that under the Law Israel had only the (Platonically fleeting and earthly) shadow of coming goods, but not the projection in this world (eikōn) of celestial, eternal, perfect realities which have now come with Christ the High Priest (9 : 11, reading 'which have come' instead of the less likely variant 'which are to come' reflected in the *futurorum bonorum* of the Latin Vulgate). We share in a heavenly calling (3 : 1) which will be perfected in the future, and in a salvation which is not a transitory, earthly one but an eternal one

(5 : 10). By faith we already have our title-deed to realities hoped for (11 : 1, taking the word hypostasis in the sense of 'title-deed' which is attested in Greek papyri).

Significantly, in Hb. 6 : 4-6 'tasting the *heavenly* gift' is parallel with 'having a share in holy spirit' and with 'tasting the word of God and the powers of the *coming* age': all of them can be had in this life and, once had, can still be lost in this life, although they belong to the coming age. They come to us through the word of God and the sacraments, which are, in categories derived from Platonism, the earthly projections of eikones of a salvation which in chapters 8 and 9 of Hebrews, with the author's use of Jewish exposition and Platonising speculation, is expressed as one perfected in the heavenly sphere by the exalted Christ. In that part of the epistle the author mingles imagery of Christ reigning in glory at the right hand of the heavenly throne with that of the High Priest carrying out his work of salvation in the heavenly sanctuary. The sanctuary or tabernacle in which he does so is heavenly (8 : 1), 'pitched by God, not by man' (8 : 2), and is thus of a transcendent order in which the liturgy performed by Christ (symbolically representing His death and ascension and enthronement in glory) achieves a salvation which is eternal and enduring (5 : 9; 9 : 12), in the place of God's real dwelling in majesty (8 : 1), which is also the place of man's perfect and eternal union with God (12 : 22-24). He has made available to us eternal happiness with God in accordance with our heavenly calling (3 : 1). If we have been 'cleansed with clean water' (10 : 22), we can already taste the gift of heavenly salvation, but we can also lose it subsequently in this world (6 : 4). we still have to seek after the personal holiness 'without which no one shall see the Lord' (12 : 14). And so, according to the author of Hebrews, already in this visible world we share sacramentally in the invisible eschatological benefits of heaven, but our share will be definitive only when we have left this world of shadows for the one of heavenly realities, where we shall appear with Christ before the face of God forever.

4. THE RESURRECTION AND HEAVEN

One question not much dealt with in the New Testament is that of the relation of heaven to the resurrection of the body. In most Jewish literature of the intertestamental period resurrection, limited to the just, surely meant a restoration of the forces of bodily life (see Dn. 12 : 1-3; 2 Macc. 7 : 9-14; 12 : 43-46; Psalms of Solomon 3 : 12), but this presumably was expected in a future restoration in this world, at the end of the present age. Once heaven was accepted as the goal of all those ultimately to be saved, the matter of integrating a heavenly mode of existence in the next life with the future resurrection of the body had sooner or later to be raised. On the one hand, the tradition of the assumption of certain men of the past like Henoch, Moses and Elijah into heaven after death, or even without the intervention of death, indicated the possibility of bodily existence in heaven, and for Christians this possibility was confirmed by the ascension of the Lord into heaven after his resurrection. But on the other hand, the concept of a spiritual soul capable of an existence apart from the material body, taken together with the Hellenistic concept of heaven as a spiritual place transcending the material world, eventually made it necessary to explain how the body might rise to acquire a celestial existence in glory.

In Palestinian Judaism, less influenced by Hellenistic thought, it was difficult to see how one might enjoy the goods of the eschatological age without a body. It was precisely in this quarter, in fact, that hope in the resurrection of the body came to be especially strong, but the life to which the body would rise was looked upon generally in those circles as a life on earth in the future age rather than in heaven. In Hellenistic Judaism, on the other hand, with its concept of the soul, or of the spirit, the soul was seen to be immortal, capable of existence by itself, and occasionally even thought to have had an existence before its union with the body, while the body was seen to be material and transitory, and so of little importance for eschatological life. Indeed, the more Jewish thinkers were influenced by Hellenistic thought the less need they sensed for a future resurrection of the body. In the strongly Hellenistic Wisdom of Solomon it is the *souls* of the just that are in the hand of God and enjoy beatitude (Wis. 3 : 1-9), and it is with respect to the soul that 'their hope is full of immortality' (3 : 4, where the word 'immortality' itself is used for the first time in a book of the Old Testament). The same fundamental attitude is found in 4 Maccabees, Henoch 108, Slavic Henoch, and even some of the Essene writings, though far less consequentially than in the works of the Alexandrian Jew Philo. The Platonising theory of the spiritual and heavenly world as one grasped only by the spiritual forces of the mind, when applied by Philo in his speculations on the destiny of the soul, left little place at all in his thought for a resurrection of the material and earthly body. Josephus, *De bello judaico* 2, 8, 14, tells us that the Pharisees held that the soul exists without the body between death and the change from this age to the next, when the souls of the good will acquire another body while those of the evil will be subjected to an everlasting punishment. The Pharisees thus integrated the expectation of a kind of bodily resurrection with the principle of the immortality of the soul, but it does not appear from this that the Pharisees had really absorbed the idea of a heavenly or transcendent existence for the soul which they expected to pass into that second body, after judgement.

In nascent Christianity the resurrection of the dead became a basic tenet, announced by Jesus himself (Mk. 12 : 18-27 and parallels), but the problem of integrating it with the expectation of a specifically heavenly existence was not everywhere dealt with. In Jn. 11 : 23-26 the dialogue between Martha and Jesus shows the late Jewish belief in resurrection unto life at the end of this age, with Jesus Himself now the source of resurrection and life; the question of heaven as the destination of the bodies which will have risen is not raised. In the Synoptic Gospels the corporeality of the image of the heavenly banquet (Mt. 8 : 11; Lk. 13 : 28-29) can not be pressed. On the contrary, the existence of the just in heaven will not entail the corporeality of this world, at least, for 'when they rise from the dead they neither marry nor are given in marriage, but are like angels in heaven' (Mk. 12 : 25 and parallels). Such texts, however, do not really contend with the speculative question how the body can exist in heaven. In the Platonising concepts which the author of the Epistle to the Hebrews so consistently uses, salvation can consist only in a passage to the invisible, heavenly world where the believer will encounter God. It is perhaps because there is little room in this type of thought for reflection on the resurrection of the material body (for the reason noted above when we mentioned Philo) that the author of Hebrews does not speak of the resurrection of the dead except to mention it as a basic element of Christian doctrine. In Hebrews eschatology of the individual is an eschatology of ascension to the heavenly world rather than of resurrection from the tomb.

In the New Testament it is St Paul who finally formulated a solution to the problem of the body's participation in eternal life. In his earlier words on the resurrection in 1 Th. 4 : 13-17 he does not yet attempt such a solution. There, he states the fact of the resurrection of the dead, and the apocalyptic imagery he uses has to do with the resurrection itself; it has no speculative import, and it does not extend to a description of the condition of life after the resurrection. When he wrote that early letter, he judged it sufficient for his readers to know that the things having to do with eternal glory belong to a realm which is not of those things which are seen but of those which are unseen and which are by that very fact eternal (cf. 2 Co. 4 : 18). To the more philosophical problem of the body in a world that is heavenly rather than earthly the key furnished by St Paul is the transcendental vital force of divine spirit which the Christian acquires in baptism and which will raise him to the divine level of existence as a son of God. From the spirit come resurrection and eternal life (Rm. 8 : 10-11; cf. 2 Co. 3 : 6 and compare Jn. 6 : 33). Those of us who have the first fruits of the spirit await sonship, 'the redemption of our body' (Rm. 8 : 2; compare Lk. 20 : 36). In 1 Co. 15 the real problem is clearly stated: 'Flesh and blood can not inherit the kingdom of God, nor can corruption inherit incorruption (15 : 50). But the body of the resurrection is not merely flesh and blood with a vivifying soul or psyche as are the bodies of all men, represented by Adam, but also one with spirit or pneuma (15 : 44-45), and this is realised in the bodies of Christians because we are incorporated not only into the first Adam of dust but also into the second Adam, who is Christ: the second Adam is 'from heaven', and hence we, by the fact of our incorporation into him by baptism, are 'heavenly' (15 : 47-49). In 2 Co. 5 : 1-10 the body is spoken of in the imagery of a garment or dwelling. We long to put on the new dwelling from God, which is eternal, in heaven (5 : 1-4), and God fits us out for this by giving us already in this world the 'first instalment' or 'pledge' (arrafān) which is of the spirit (5 : 5).

The essential in our well founded hope for life in heaven, however, lies simply in our being there with Christ, the Lord (2 Co. 5 : 7-8; Phil. 1 : 23; 1 Th. 4 : 17; 5 : 10). Speculative questions having to do with the mode of existence in heaven are of secondary importance, as St. Paul himself knew, although they are useful in dealing, as in 1 Co. 15, with those who have philosophical difficulties because of the metaphysical barrier between the heavenly or spiritual and the earthly or material. Jesus Himself, in Mk. 12 : 26-27 and parallels, is little concerned with such questions; he shows us that our hope in our resurrection is founded in our faith in the God of Abraham, Isaac and Jacob, who, though they are dead to this life, live: 'He is not a God of the dead but of the living'.

Peter Stockmeier

'Models' of Heaven in Christian Religious Feeling

THE IDEA of heaven has from the beginning been part of the religious feeling of Christians, and continues to influence their existence in time and history. However, as the evidence of the Old and New Testaments themselves shows, the meaning of this kerygmatic term is not simple, a circumstance which was subsequently to lend wings to theological and spiritual interpretation, particularly since official doctrinal correction was quite rare. This meant that no limits were set to the metaphorical ornamentation of 'what no eye has seen' (Is 64 : 4 (3); 1 Cor 2 : 9), with the result that the biblical statements were modified and supplemented according to the spirit of each age. Nevertheless the character of early Christian theology, moving as it did largely within the framework of the biblical revelation, prevented subjective projections from leading religious feeling too far astray, although a good many 'models' can be explained only by reference to the current intellectual and religious background. For example, just at the beginning of the Christian era the existential experience of ancient man was characterised by the idea of the cosmos as a cavern (O. Spengler), the influence of which was more pervasive than that of natural science. How strongly in this period, as the august greatness of the Olympian gods faded, the cosmic dimension influenced religious feeling is illustrated by the worship of Mithras, whose brotherhoods gathered for ritual meals in caves with vaulted ceilings symbolising the starry heaven. Christians too continued to be influenced by the ancient picture of the world when they made theological statements, and this mythological background must be borne in mind not least in the case of the metaphor of heaven.

It is therefore not surprising that we should come across different versions of the idea of heaven in the course of history. If we call these 'models', we are using the word not in the sense of an accurate copy, but in the language of analogy, to mean 'a humanly produced simple "structural form" as a cipher for a trans-individual specific entity'.[1] Not even for the revealed fact 'heaven' do conceptual models derived from faith claim to be definitive; rather, they reflect the awareness of one period, and stimulate continued enquiry. The term 'heaven' is thus an ideal example of the historical nature of theological language.

1. THE SPHERE OF GOD'S EXISTENCE

The post-apostolic communities on the whole did not move far from the biblical statements in their descriptions of heaven. At first the writing of the period, with its paraenetic bias, does not discuss heaven as such; biblical texts are quoted where appropriate and the reality of heaven is taken for granted in the argument. The cosmic view of the world prevalent in the surrounding culture also had an influence. It is not hard to see that the theological statements are being made in a context dominated by the ancient picture of the world which treats heaven as some kind of 'place'. This topological structure is based on belief in the division of the world into three parts: heaven, the abode of the gods, on top; a corresponding underworld; with the earth, floating on water, in the middle.

This spherical picture of the world was accepted by Christians, if sometimes modified, as when Cosmas Indicopleustes (middle of the sixth century) rejected the spherical hypothesis of Ptolemy (second century) for a cubic model. Otherwise the Church Fathers show little interest in cosmological speculations, even in commentary on the six days of creation, and so show a measure of independence from the current picture of the world. Despite their entanglement with contemporary ideas of the cosmos, the primary purpose of statements about heaven in early Christian literature is theological. This intention is shown in the numerous texts which describe God as the creator of the world and therefore of heaven too: this gives particular prominence to the idea of salvation. Particularly in view of the influence of so many mystery cults, the belief in the exaltation of Christ as the pledge of one's own resurrection and the guarantee of eternal life acquires fundamental importance. Characteristic is the description by the author of 1 Clement, with a direct reference to 1 Cor 2 : 9 (1 Clem 34, 8-35, 2), of the future blessings of salvation as guaranteed by God. Heaven is regarded as God's sphere, and is described from the point of view of the salvation of man: life in immortality, joy in justice, truth in frankness, moderation in sanctification (1 Clem 35 : 2). What is noticeable about this description is the feedback from the Christian's existence in 'faith-knowledge', though this had to develop its existential potential against the real possibility of martyrdom. Communion with God is thus the goal of life and the content of that reality for which heaven is a label. In the description of these blessings of salvation, that is, following the move from personal language about God to material descriptions, it is not uncommon to find a comparison with earthly values, and even the idea of an exchange in the sense of a surpassing.

Despite its diversification into a multiplicity of goods of salvation, the assimilation of heaven and God has its roots in the personal. This perspective predominates in the understanding of the early Church, and it is in its terms that spatial and material conceptions of heaven must be interpreted, even, or especially, in a period when the assumptions of ancient natural science had fallen into disuse. Here already, too, we see how much such 'models' depend on the current image of God.

2. APOCALYPTIC ELABORATION

In accordance with its conception of itself, apocalyptic always sought to unveil the mystery of heaven, and is largely responsible for Christian ideas on the subject. Apocalyptic was influenced by the relevant inter-testamental literature and given legitimacy by the canonical Apocalypse, and strengthened its influence still further when believers had become convinced of the postponement of the parousia. It is easy to see how in the process it took over those elements and attitudes, for example in 1 Enoch, which encouraged the tendency to elaborate the next world. However, in contrast to a work like the Revelation to John, interest is no longer concentrated on describing the victory of Christ, but in portraying heaven and its conditions. What is generally only hinted at in New Testament writing is lavishly articulated in these apocalypses, for example the idea of a number of levels. In imitation of the book of Enoch, for example, the Assumption of Isaiah depicts heaven as divided into seven ascending regions, the highest of which is filled with wonderful light and angels without number (9 : 6). The author of the Apocalypse of Paul portrays a definitely supra-terrestrial world when he makes his heaven contain paradise and the holy city, two independent motifs. The book starts from Paul's ecstasy as reported in 2 Cor 12, and the apostle then passes through the various meadows, enters paradise through a gate, sees from above the earth with its surrounding ocean, and is finally allowed to gaze on the high altar, the curtain and the throne itself. What the authors of these productions are really doing is depicting the various regions of heaven as vividly as possible to meet human needs, and portraying blessedness with motifs from the Jewish tradition or even ancient mythology, as instanced by the picture of Elysium.

What is presented here is a 'model' of heaven built up from various traditions which answers the hope of an after-life of a fundamentally pessimistic age. The tribulations of this existence, experienced in one's own life or observed in the decline of the world, are caught up and transformed into a heavenly splendour. The imaginative embellishment acts as a compensation for joys foregone in earthly life, all the more in that the unjust receive their punishment. The others, however, as the Christian Sibyl promises around A.D. 150 'who have performed works of virtue and, walking in piety, have kept a good conscience, are taken up by angels and brought from the stream of burning fire to the light, into a life full of bliss and joy, where the eternal path of the mighty God leads and triple springs of wine and milk and honey flow. The earth is the same for all and, not divided by walls and barriers, now brings forth of itself even more fruits: life is shared in wealth which has no owners! There are no servants there and no masters; there there are no princes, and all are equal before the Most High'.[2] With such promises the Christian Sibylline oracles swell into full-blown social criticism. They produce a picture of a heavenly community which is clearly contrasted with earthly conditions in the Roman Empire and by this time has a revolutionary ring. The directness of its criticism certainly gave this visionary model a purchase on the actual situation, and appeals from Church Fathers to make earth a heaven[3] also illustrate the suggestive power of apocalyptic ideas of the next world. On the other hand, it must also be remembered that the apocalyptic model of heaven is largely dominated by a system of order such as the one produced from neo-Platonic assumptions by Pseudo-Dionysus in his doctrine of the hierarchies.

3. THE CITY OF GOD

One of the most enduring influences was the image of the city of God, a 'model' of heaven which, despite its connection with the next world, is full of this-worldly detail.[4] Ever since men adopted the city form of settlement, the concept of the city had been associated with a range of feelings among which community, security, home and culture predominate: as a political universe the phenomenon of the city often takes on even a religious quality. Naturally, in the biblical view Jerusalem has a unique status, and not just as the historical centre of the people of Israel; numerous scriptural statements go beyond the earthly function of the city to describe it as part of the salvation of the last times (Rev 20 : 10-27 etc.). In Christian thought too, Jerusalem was certainly not just a symbol of the world to come, since it was often used as the ideal of the life of faith, but nevertheless it was only its connection with eschatological hopes that preserved its force. The tension between the security of home (*polis*) and being a stranger (*paroikia*) has been a feature of Christian existence in the world from the beginning, and this dialectic also left its mark on the Christian attitude to history. It was Augustine (d. 430) who most enduringly gave expression to this belief and characterised the nature of membership of God's city, not least in deliberate contrast with the intrinsically religious tradition of Rome. It is significant, however, that it is not in his profound historical speculation, the *De Civitate Dei,* that the bishop of Hippo first takes up the image of the city. He introduces it earlier in his *De catechizandis rudibus,* when he talks about the spiritual characteristics of that earthly empire and of the famous city of Jerusalem, 'which is meant to be a model for that free city which is called the heavenly Jerusalem'. After an etymological explanation of the name Jerusalem as 'manifestation of peace', he describes the citizens of this city as 'all the consecrated people who have ever been, are now or one day will be, and all the consecrated spirits who serve God in the heavenly heights in pious adoration and refuse to imitate the impudent arrogance of the devil and his angels'.[5]

The Christological orientation of this model is expressed when Christ is subsequently described as the king of the city. As early as the first catechetical instruction, the image of the city serves as a model of heaven, a statement which Augustine in his historical writing expresses in dynamic terms, in the idea of God's citizens pressing towards this goal through the ages. They reach their fulfilment in the vision and apprehension of God, who is himself the source and substance of blessedness. Through all mankind's involvement in the vicissitudes of history, Augustine picks out this possibility and presents it as the essence of blessedness. 'He will be the end of our longing, he who can be gazed on without end, loved without surfeit and praised without weariness.'[6]

There can be no doubt that this interpretation of eschatological fulfilment centres the city of God on God and the vision of him enjoyed by the blessed. The background to this spiritualisation comes from contemporary tendencies in philosophy, which are concerned with the rise of man and the knowledge of the One and go beyond images imprisoned in material things. The degree to which this reduction to knowledge, truth and God enriched Augustine's thought is illustrated in the sensitive dialogue the great theologian had with his mother in Ostia as she waited for death. Hear he outlines and ascent beyond all sensible things, beyond the sights and sounds of this world, to a silent openness to His word which is direct perception of the God who is eternal life.[7] While Augustine too starts from the premiss that there are various degrees in the vision of God, this does not prevent him from regarding the city of the blessed as a true community, and so the picture of heaven as the city which is above is retained. At the same time the reduction of the idea to the vision of God which the blessed enjoy strips it of that picturesque vividness which was a feature of the apocalyptic models and opens the way for an understanding of heaven as a new quality of community between God and perfected man. Despite the strong and persistent influence of Augustine's model of the beatific vision on the theology of the middle ages, the image of the heavenly Jerusalem, the city of God model, nevertheless continued to live in religious feeling with undiminished force. This symbol had a particularly strong attraction for the Christianised Germanic tribes. Imagined as a structure, richly built, this motif fulfils all human hopes and expectations. Otto of Freising (d. 1158), the medieval historiographer, takes up the picture of the book of Revelation, in which this city 'is built of pure gold, the foundations of all sorts of precious jewels, each of its twelve gates out of a pearl, and the streets are paved with sheets of pure gold like transparent glass: we can imagine how magnificent our life would be in this heavenly fatherland! For if it is beautiful and magnificent when taken in the literal sense, how much more beautiful and magnificent does it appear understood in a spiritual sense!'[8] The image of the heavenly city is one of the most vivid conceptions of eschatological hope, and its force is not diminished by the idea of spiritual vision. It was also easy to draw parallels from it with the earthly Church, as when the same Otto of Freising sees the hierarchical degrees of the clergy as modelled on the ordering of the heavenly court (caelestis curia).[9] In this way the heavenly model, constructed by Pseudo-Dionysus and adopted by medieval canonists, helped to legitimise the structure of ecclesiastical authority. The unique role of the papacy, of the successor of Peter, was expressed in this application in the function of the apostle Peter as keeper of the gate and custodian of the keys of this heavenly city. There is a characteristic illustration of this attitude in the scene at the Synod of Whitby (663) when the Anglo-Saxon king Oswiu, faced with a choice between Irish local customs and Roman practice, decided for Peter so that there should be someone there to open to him when he came to heaven's gate.[10] In the Freising hymn to St. Peter, which opens the history of German hymnology towards the end of the ninth century, and celebrates the authority of the keeper of the gate of heaven, this feeling spreads out into the domain of popular piety. Inevitably the hymn recalls the role of his successor in Rome, the city which itself steadily worked its way into the minds of the faithful as the urbs sacra, the holy city. The figure of Peter the prince of the apostles formed the basis for the assimilation of the city of the popes to the heavenly Jerusalem. And although the crusades forcefully reinstated the earthly Jerusalem in the consciousness of medieval Christendom and even the cruciform ground-plan seems to have influenced many cities of this period,[11] the correspondence between heavenly city and worldly authority reached its climax in the doctrine of the power of the keys vested in the successor of Peter.

4. ECCLESIA TRIUMPHALIS

The symbol of the power of the keys in itself forms a link with another idea of heaven, the *ecclesia triumphans*. Quite clearly, this is an image derived from ecclesiology which expresses the eschatological perfection of the wandering people of God. When alongside the concepts 'heavenly', 'transcendent' or 'cosmic' there appears the description of the Church as 'triumphant', a contrast is being made with the embattled Church on earth. It is true that the description of Christian existence in the world as a contest, at first means the struggle with the forces of evil which the believer has to endure. This was a common metaphor in the ancient world, and the author of the letter from the Roman community to Corinth uses it when he talks of the athletes of the recent past, and mentions Peter, who, by his witness, had reached the due place of glory.[12] With the experience of martyrdom this theme increased in importance. For those who bore witness by their blood, the endurance of suffering meant heavenly glory: it is the martyrs who triumph with Christ, who passed through death and resurrection. In this cult of martyrdom the influence of the liturgy in the book of Revelation (6 : 9) is unmistakable, and it too contributed to the growth of the idea of the Church triumphant. The amalgamation of spiritual mission and political interests of course gave this image an authoritarian dimension, and its triumphalist cast worked back from the eschatological victory of Christ to feed the Church's vision of herself in history. Thomas Aquinas (d. 1274) used phrases from Augustine's teaching on the city of God to stress the difference between an *ecclesia militans* on earth and an *ecclesia triumphans* in heaven.[13] The increasing frequency of this distinction from the middle of the twelfth century reflects the situation of a period absorbed in the movement of the crusades and shaken by militant disputes within the *societas*. However, the this-worldly struggle of the Church is matched by an other-worldly fulfilment in heaven which is characterised through and through by triumphalism. This glory is the reward for all the burdens and privations the Church militant has to endure. This triumphalist concept of heaven inevitably recalls the triumphal processions of the Roman emperors in ancient Rome, which was also evoked in other contexts in the middle ages. The principle of correspondence between 'above' and 'below' also led to attempts to implement the 'model', not only in the ecclesiastical, but also in the political sphere.[14] In theology the idea of the Church triumphant was closely attached to the concept of the kingdom of God, and one of the chief effects of this was to give vigorous encouragement to the political ambitions of the Church of Rome.

5. HEAVEN AS AN ACADEMY

The idea of heaven as an academy took an original form in the history of theology. Already in the description in 1 Cor 13 : 9-12 of our knowledge in this life as only fragmentary it is made clear that at the fulfilment this obstacle will disappear, and that heavenly existence will include full knowledge. As is well known, the contrast between faith and Gnosis was both a burden and a boon for Christian thought in every century, but the justification of knowledge as against faith was often based on this eschatological promise. It is notable that in numerous Gnostic systems the heavenly goal is described in terms of perfect knowledge.[15] Now, in the wake of the attempts to establish theology as a science, abstruse speculation produced the model of heaven as an academy. The idea had already been current in Judaism. The earthly school in which scholars and pupils met to study the scriptures was held to have a counterpart in a heavenly academy which housed the order of rabbis.[16] An important feature for the Christian adoption of the idea was the existence of a connection between the disputing teachers above and below, in that the souls of the earthly rabbis ascended to the heavenly school to learn there. The concept of theology as a science developed by scholasticism obviously connects with this idea. In Thomas Aquinas' definition: 'Sacred doctrine is a science because it proceeds from principles known by the light of a higher science, namely the knowledge of God and the blessed' (*Sacra doctrina est scientia quia procedit ex principiis notis lumine superioris scientiae, quae scilicet est scientia Dei et beatorum*).[17] The absolute, fundamental truths represent the knowledge of God and the blessed, which is made known in revelation and is accessible to man in faith. This inevitably gives theology a subordinate status; it ranks as a *scientia subalterna*, over-shadowed by a higher intellectual enterprise, heaven as an academy.

In art this model received a famous embodiment in the Stanza della Segnatura of the Vatican Palace, where Raphael (d. around 1520) depicted the glorification of the Christian mystery. To the representatives of theology on earth there corresponds in heaven the massed academy of blessed doctors. In spite the narrowing of the theological concept of science it implies, this model illustrates in a unique way the perfection of knowledge.

6. PARADISE

On the principle that the end is like the beginning, theological reflection linked the beginning and the end of man and so turned the idea of paradise into a powerful 'model' of heaven.[18] Questions about the fate of the dead led at first to different answers. The Jewish Christian tradition produced the ideas of a resurrection and a kingdom lasting a thousand years, while in a Hellenistic context there was greater emphasis on the fate of the individual immediately after death. Paradise was an important topic in this lively discussion, though opinions about it varied. With the postulation of an intermediate state (*interim refrigerium*), a clear grading was introduced into conceptions of the final state: only the martyrs were thought worthy of immediate entry into the heavenly paradise. To this extent the description of paradise was also heavily influenced by the idea of union with Christ, though many metaphorical elements from the Jewish and Hellenistic worlds were also included which strongly emphasised the material aspect, especially as the topographical identification of paradise remained current. This attitude also dominates the medieval vision of paradise, to which Dante (d. 1321)—more effectively than theology—gave classical expression. Here above all, through the imagery of a work of art and the framework of an antique cosmography, we get a glimpse of the fulfilment promised to man.

In the history of Christianity the metaphor of heaven has crystallised in many ways the human hopes which grow out of the faith. The resulting 'models' were products of revelation and at the same time interwoven with contemporary cosmologies, and they finally converge in the promise of a new heaven and a new earth. They stand openly side by side in Christian religious feeling like the parables of Jesus, or they succeed one another, so proving their capacity for renewal. Since God is always the focus of their metaphorical statement, they free themselves from mythical fetters and yet do not degenerate into secularised projections because their ultimate image for the core of the kerygmatic term 'heaven' is union with him.

Translated by Francis McDonagh

Notes

1. J. Auer 'Die Bedeutung der "Modell-Idee" für die "Hilfsbegriffe" des katholischen Dogmas' J. Ratzinger and H. Fries (ed.) *Einsicht und Glaube* (Freiburg, Basle, Vienna 1962) pp. 259-279, quotation from p. 267. General information related to heaven is provided by P. Bernard 'Ciel' *Dict. Théol Cath* 2 (1905) 2474-2511; L. Brémond *Le Ciel. Ses Joies—Ses Splendeurs* (Paris, 10th ed. 1925); A. Stange *Das frühchristliche Kirchengebäude als Bild des Himmels* (Cologne 1950); N. Wicki *Die Lehre von der himmlischen Seligkeit in der mittelalterlichen Scholastik von Petrus Lombardus bis Thomas von Aquin* Studia Fribugensia, NF 9 (Fribourg 1954); U. Simon *Heaven in the Christian Tradition* (London 1958); R. Hugues *Heaven and Hell in Western Art* (London 1968); R. Greshake *Stärker als der Tod* (Mainz 1976); J. Ratzinger *Eschatologie—Tod und ewiges Leben* Kleine katholische Dogmatik IX (Regensburg 1977).

2. *Orac. Sibill.* 2, 314-323 (Hennecke-Schneemelcher II, pp. 508-509—translation from the German).

3. Cf. John Chrysostom *Hom. 19, 5 in Mt* (PG 57,279).

4. See N. Schneider *'Civitas Caelestis'—Studien zum Jerusalem-Symbolismus* dissertation (Münster 1969).

5. Augustine *De cat. rud.* 20 (Krüger 42).

6. Augustine *De civ. Dei* 22, 30 (CCL 48,863).

7. Augustine *Conf.* 9,10 (CSEL 33,217).

8. Otto *Chronik* 8,26 (Schmidt-Lammers, p. 652).

9. *Ibid.* 8,29 (Schmidt-Lammers, p. 651).

10. Bede *Eccles. Hist.* III, 25 (Colgrave-Mynors, p. 306).

11. Cf. W. Müller *Die heilige Stadt. Roma quadrata, himmlisches Jerusalem und die Mythe vom Weltnabel* (Stuttgart 1961) 53ff.

12. 1 Clem 5 : 1-4 (Bihlmeyer-Schneemelcher, p. 38).

13. S.Th. II. 10, 2, 4 and *passim*.

14. There is an impressive example of this in Byzantine imperial ceremonial; see O. Treitinger, *Die oströmische Kaiserund Reichsidee nach ihrer Gestaltung im höfischen Zeremoniell* (Jena 1938, reprint Darmstadt 1956).

15. Cf. W. Bousset 'Die Himmelsreise der Seele' *Archiv f. Religionswissenschaft* 4 (1901), 136-69 (reprint Darmstadt 1960).

16. H. Bietenhard *Die himmlische Welt im Urchristentum und Spätjudentum*, Wiss, Unters. s. NT, 2 (Tübingen 1951) pp. 186ff.

17. S.Th. I : 1, 2.

18. Cf. R. R. Grimm *Paradisus coelestis—Paradisus terrestris. Zur Auslegungsgeschichte de Paradieses im Abendland bis um 1200 (Medium aevum* XXXIII, Munich 1977).

Robert Favre

Various Accounts of Heaven in the French 'Age of Enlightenment'

'THE CHURCH condemns all those who let their imaginations run riot in this sort of thing and who have the presumption to set themselves outside the simple truths of dogma.'

These words were written in 1773 by a Jesuit, Francois de Feller, in his *Catechisme philosophique* as a reminder to 'those who in matters of doctrine think they are different from other people'. He criticised those 'over-zealous souls' for indulging in lurid and detailed descriptions of hell. His criticisms applied to quite a number of his fellow clerics whose enthusiasm for arousing what they called 'salutary fears' encouraged a rhetoric that was already too deeply ingrained in them. It is known that they were also attacked by the 'enlightened' French philosophers for the kind of religion which, founded on the twin fears of death and damnation, leads to the enslavement of man; but what are less well-known in 'this sort of thing' are the arguments put foward about the nature of heaven. Now these contributed as much material to one side as the other, deist or atheist, in the anti-Christian debate. Yet throughout all the accounts, criticisms and images of eternal bliss that they employed we discover the very difficulty we have ourselves—that of expressing in ordinary language what it means to share in the life of God and to attain perfect union with Him. So it may be useful to recall the particular imbalances, aberrations and excesses that typified eighteenth-century France, especially as they might well even today shape a Christian's view of salvation and either give rise to understandable renunciation or a too fearful way of living.[1]

These brief observations, based on texts I believe to be representative, only serve to illustrate a wide variety of beliefs which involve 'presumption' and are far from the 'simple truths of dogma'. The reader should look upon this essay, with its limited terms of reference, as a framework for a more critical study.

Let us not waste time on naïve ideas, especially those which attempt to locate heaven within any particular system of the Universe. It was that same Feller who ridiculed 'certain theologians' who placed hell 'in the innermost regions of the earth', and then Voltaire 'for not believing in heaven because there was no proof one existed on the moon, on Jupiter or on Venus', (*Dictionnaire philosophique art. 'Ciel'*) yet, after he had touched on the hypothesis that heaven 'could not have any precise location', Feller decided in the end that it was 'a special abode' . . . 'somewhere'. The word 'heaven' does seem to encourage a spatial way of thinking. Another critic of Voltaire's, the Benedictine, Dom Chaudon, defines 'heaven' in his *Anti-Dictionnaire philosophique* as 'somewhere, far above all the planets, where the Supreme Being receives the homage of the just whose virtue He rewards'. One can see the social and cultural influences in this passage—a feudal God enthroned in a celestial Court. We project our own ideas of relationships into any idealised society and in so far as we do this, our descriptions of heaven are not politically neutral!

More characteristically, however, we find through all their sermons, treatise and meditations various manifestations of *pessimistic* or *anguished* Christianity. Whenever heaven is described as a place of astonishing delights, where happiness is perfect and everlasting, then all human experience here on earth is consequently devalued—all existence in a world that 'is ridden with sin and misery, a vale of mourning and tears, a land of the living-dead, full of obstacles and suffering, an accursed exile where the soulful inhabitants do nothing but bewail their fate, curse the day and blaspheme against the "Author of their existence"'. Thus preached Bridaine (1701-1767) in a *Sermon sur le Paradis*; he was a missionary priest who journeyed all over France with great acclaim for forty years. *We* cannot be sure—like Charles Péguy—that not only our Lady of Chartres but even our Lady of Paris as well are eternally in God's presence as double evidence of mankind's achievement! But we must be wary of any account of heaven that turns it into a refuge or fills it with compensatory riches, for such a view undervalues life on earth. Well before Marx and Nietzche, Voltaire, Diderot and d'Holbach vehemently countered any view of heaven that glorified it as our one and only 'home', the very antithesis of this earth. If some people place all their hope, particularly their Christian hope, in building an earthly kingdom, surely it is because for a very long time, well before the eighteenth and nineteenth centuries, a depressed clergy had contrariwise instructed their people to attend to nothing but 'the life beyond'. Perhaps one should now ask if this stiff indifference to 'everything that is not eternal, and the languid distaste of these precious souls is not more indicative of a schizophrenic mentality or one of those fringe groups found in a changing society. But in the eighteenth century that spirituality which comprised a contempt for the world and 'a holy desire for death' was carried to such lengths that it should be ascribed to a collective failure of nerve in a country faced with the spiritual decline of a long-established Christianity.[2]

There is another view of heaven in which psychological and/or sociological influences could have been at work. In living out the specific encounter with God, does the person find himself in a one-to-one relationship which excludes all others? To read writings such as Nicole's, on whom countless readers, Jansenist and non-Jansenist, were brought up in the seventeenth and eighteenth centuries, we find sentences like: 'it was to live in eternal solitude with God that man was created.' Nicole himself states 'The communion of saints will not disturb their solitude in any way . . .'.[3]

Sometimes too, for Christians, and even for deists, eternal life appears to be the individual's enjoyment of rewards given by the sovereign judge, who metes out all reward and punishment. Of course we can in such places discern a desire to emphasise God's infinite distance; only he and his gifts can satisfy man's heart's desire. But is there not also in these stark and inept accounts the grave neglect of communion with others? There is a sort of spiritual individualism that has long been a feature of preaching about withdrawal, preparing for death and salvation. A heaven conceived in such terms does not reflect the promised sharing at the divine 'banquet': nor is such an imposing encounter with God a 'Catholic' idea. The Church as the body of Christ could be forgotten or obscured like this only within the context of a way of thinking which is too close to so-called bourgeois individualism. And there is a sentimental version of a similar tendency: here the emphasis is on reunion after death with one's loved ones to the point where the sense of beatitude within the context of the Church is likewise obscured. This is certainly the case in the unorthodox enough novels of the time; consider the ending of Abbé Prévost's *Cleveland*, one of the greatest successes of the age, or Jean-Jacques Rousseau's ending of *La Nouvelle Heloise*. But the correspondence and the memoirs of the day also show how important this hope of seeing departed friends, spouses or relatives was to religious people. Among the more noteworthy were President Dugas, Moreau, who was the King's official historian, and Necker and his wife. Such a heartfelt impulse is irreproachable. Nevertheless we should beware of the sort of emotion that lies behind such a wish;

when it tends to enfold hope in a dream of emotional bliss, heaven becomes restricted to a small circle of close friends who are then no longer God's guests, but our own elect. On the other hand, this urgent need to make the community in heaven an exclusive one can reveal other ambiguities. To limit it to a 'little flock' stems as much from a boundless respect for God's supreme power as from a preference for *élitism*. In another passage in his *Essais de morale*, Nicole drew up a long list of categories of people to be excluded from heaven, and the Jesuits, opposed by Nicole's uncompromising followers, had great difficulty in maintaining the traditional theory that pagans could possibly be saved: in the Age of Enlightenment that belief was held to be heretical, to the great scandal of the 'enlightened' spirits. Without going into details of that long controversy which was noted in particular for the row the Sorbonne had with Marmontel over his *Bélisaire*, we may recall that Julie made this plea to the readers of *La Nouvelle Héloise*: 'Do not let us do any of the Devil's awful work: let us not open the gates of hell so easily to our own kind'. And it was precisely on account of this form of intolerance that ever since her youth Madame Roland had lost her faith. In 1743, in his *Traité du vrai mérite de l'homme* which ran through scores of editions, the Maître de Claville, an admirable Christian moralist, asked quite plainly: 'Does the censure of the damned add anything to the happiness of the elect?' 'Of course it does' the Archbishop of Lyon, Malvin de Montazet, replies when, under the cover of promises that are 'so comforting to the souls of the faithful'—souls who remain faithful in these times of unbelief—he assures them that they will share in eternal vengeance of God on his enemies. And he wrote in his *Instruction pastorale* in 1776, 'We shall execute the fearsome sentence that will have been pronounced on the impious.' Previously, a Benedictine, Dom Sensaric had preached on the great revenge of the just: 'And so the just will render contempt for contempt. . . . And so they will bathe in the blood of the sinners who have fed on their tears.' What a curious way for heaven to communicate with hell! There we have the weird fruits of man's resentment!

It is very difficult to describe in what heaven's beatitude consists. Those who try to do it come up against three kinds of obstacle: *narcissism, intellectualism* and *academicism*.

In the first instance, the 'just man' finds happiness in his own sufficiency. This is how Rousseau described beatitude: 'as the lovely remembrance of all the good we have done down here' (*Confessions* Book XII); and if we refer to his description of this ecstasy in fifth of his *Rêveries du promeneur solitaire*, we will notice that in this anticipation of sublime happiness, 'one is sufficient unto oneself like God'. Here we see that the 'happiness that is complete, perfect and full' is not to be *with* God, but *like* God. There is no doubt that Rousseau's religion may have had other facets, but seen in this light, we can understand exactly what one could call, after Malraux, 'the need for deity'. The pleasure of realising one is immortal, the contentment of the just man who awaits his reward and believes it is deserved, the hope of the bereaved who sigh for reunion with loved ones in eternity, the plea of the man appalled by his own imperfections and limitations, however nobly expressed, all revere the profoundly narcissistic character of the 'old Adam' who is still to be converted. Then there is another related trap: intellectualism. Perhaps discussions on heavenly bliss are more subject to this than to somewhat sentimental or sensual treatment for we know it is by metaphor that we speak of enjoyment, delight and pleasure. On the other hand, is it not enough to make heaven the place where we see and know everything perfectly—the light of complete understanding into which the soul enters? And so, when we are invited by the image in the Gospels to a full sharing at the banquet/feast, in a communion of mutual joy with others, the person is often portrayed as a solitary intellect, and knowledge eclipses love. 'We shall see everything, and the reason for everything', Bridaine said, but at least he went on to remind his readers how lovely it is for the whole being to share in the life of God. However, this sort of thinking is quite pervasive. It is to be found, for instance, in Fontenelle, in his eulogy for a learned academician who, if Fontenelle is to be believed, 'regarded his body as the cloak which hid eternal truth from him'—a rather platonic idea—and who waited impatiently to pass 'from out the deepest shadows of ignorance into the perfect light of understanding'. In fact, this yearning to see and know everything is blended with the pessimism we have already mentioned, but it is surprising to find it again in a scholar. There are other examples of this, when this emphasis on the intellect, separated from the worship of God and the communion of saints, conceals a subtle streak of narcissism.

However, all discussions on heaven are prone to become fixed in the way all accounts of utopia tend to do. Not that it is at all easy to think up a pure utopia; so it is liable to become caught up in a fictional flight of fantasy that seizes upon a threat, a flaw or an intrusion in it, as in *Cleveland*; or else it is made more lively, as in *Candide*, by giving it contemporary political relevance. What can be drier or more sterile, more conventional and academic than to talk about either utopia or heaven. Total rationality, perfect comprehension and harmony all entail a repetitive monotony as bland as those vast classical tableaux which depict existence in the Elysian fields. Even when the writer conjures up streams of endless delight and hymns of joy that rise in triumph, boredom sets in. The almighty is no longer the source of all life, but an idol set up before worshippers who are either entranced or disenchanted. Shortly before he died, Voltaire explored the idea of life after death in a poem

The Visionary; it is probably in parody of Dante. He is quickly horrified by the sight of the damned; so he moves on to the abode of the blessed, only to find that 'this Elysium and its chill beauty' is no better. He is 'immediately revolted by it' and to escape from the tedium he delivers himself up to the sombre figure of The Void. There we have, if not his last word, at least the expression of one of Voltaire's besetting tendencies. In that same year, 1778, just two centuries ago, a painter died; it was Lantara. As he lay on his deathbed, he was promised that he would soon see God face to face for ever. 'What' he asked, 'and never in profile?'

It is in a Protestant philosopher, D. R. Boullier, and in Père Bridaine that we find the least disappointing descriptions of heaven's beatitude. Boullier, still too near the man-centredness of the deists, and many a Christian writer, 'takes as his basic assumption that the human soul is immensely fertile and forever receptive to illumination, virtue and new pleasure, etc.' and he writes, 'I know of no image that gladdens my heart more than that of a path of infinite progress towards perfection for all fortunate enough to comprehend it; quite apart from being comforting and flattering, it has the great appeal of being most probably true!'[4]

Père Bridaine is full of naive and laboured images that try to transpose the energy of this life into terms of eternity, but eventually he asserts a view that is strictly God-centred: 'No, all the longing of the hart that thirsts after cool streams to slake its parched throat, all the raging of a rapid torrent swollen by abundant rains as it falls into its element, all the momentum of a huge rock breaking loose from a mountain peak and hurtling down into the depths of a valley, all the force of a fire that erupts from its underground chamber to find the open air, all these are but the faint impressions of the fervour, zeal and unutterable rapture that draw the saints towards God, their centre'.[5]

Thank God the eighteenth century gave us the 'Alleluia' chorus of Handel's *Messiah* and the 'Sanctus' from Mozart's *Mass in C*, and the Lux Perpetua from his *Requiem*; for we hardly ever hear a sermon on Paradise now—and should we regret it? Of course, there are many pitfalls and we could uncover yet more. Bridaine is now forgotten; he was a popular preacher who knew how to make fine ladies and scholars listen to him as attentively as the people in the country parishes, but it is his vision that is the least awkward; it is a vision of the indescribable reality which is the goal of all Christian hope.[5]

Translated by A. and G. Rochford

Notes

1. Jean Fagre, the late lamented expert on the eighteenth century has said that the philosophers of the Enlightenment 'put forward for the first time, at least in their modern form, questions which apply to us nowadays'.

2. See the articles of M. de Certeau and L. Coignet in *Le Mepris du monde dans la tradition spirituelle occidentale* (Paris 1965) and R. Favre *La Mort au siècle des Lumières*, Ch. 4 (Lyon 1978).

3. *Essais de Morale*, IV, 218: in *Traité des quatre fins dernières* (ed. 1696).

4. *Essai philosophique sur l'âme des bêtes*, 2nd ed. (Amsterdam 1737) II, 43.

5. *Sermons*, 2nd ed. (Avignon, 1827) I, 328-329.

James H. Cone

The Meaning of Heaven in
the Black Spirituals

I am a poor pilgrim of sorrow.
I'm in this world alone.
No hope in this world for tomorrow.
I'm trying to make heaven my home.

Although nineteenth-century North American black slaves believed
that the God of Jesus Christ was involved in the historical liberation of
oppressed people from bondage, the continued existence of slavery
seemed to contradict that belief. If God is omnipotent and is in control of
human history, how can his goodness be reconciled with human servitude? If God has the power to deliver black people from the evil of
slavery as he delivered Moses from Pharoah's army, Daniel from the
lion's den, and the Hebrew children from the fiery furnace, why then are
black slaves still subject to the rule of white masters? Why are we still
living in wretched conditions when God could end this evil thing with one
righteous stroke?

These are hard questions, and they are still relevant today. In the
history of theology and philosophy, these questions are the core of the
'problem of evil'; and college and university professors have spent many
hours debating them. But black slaves did not have the opportunity to
investigate the problem of suffering in the luxury of a seminar room with
all the comforts of modern living. They encountered suffering in the
cotton fields of Georgia, Arkansas and Mississippi. They had to deal with
the absurdities of human existence under whip and pistol. Every time
they opened their eyes and visualised the contradictions of their en-

vironment, they realised that they were 'rolling through an unfriendly world'. How could a good and powerful God be reconciled with white masters and overseers? What explanation could the Holy One of Israel give for allowing the existence of an ungodly slave institution? The answer to these questions lies in the concept of heaven, which is the dominant idea in the black religious experience as expressed in the slave songs of the nineteenth century.

The concept of heaven in black religion has not been interpreted rightly. Most observers have defined the black religious experience ex-clusively in terms of slaves longing for heaven, as if that desire was unrelated to their earthly liberation. It has been said that the concept of heaven served as an opiate for black slaves, making for docility and submission. It may be that part of this charge is related to the outmoded cosmology of the spirituals. Their old-fashioned 'world pictures' can blind critics to the message of a people seeking expression amid the dehumanisation of slavery. It is like discarding the Bible and its message as irrelevant because the biblical writers had a three-storied conception of the universe. While not all biblical and systematic theologians agree with Rudolf Bultmann's method of 'demythologisation' as the way to solve the problem (among others) of biblical cosmology, most would agree that he is correct in his insistence that the gospel message is not invalidated by its pre-scientific world-picture. A similar perspective can illumine the heaven theme in the spirituals.

Let me admit then that the black slaves' picture of the world is not to be defended as a viable scientific analysis of reality; that the language of heaven was a white concept given to black slaves in order to make them obedient and submissive; that the image of the Promised Land, where 'the streets are pearl and the gates are gold', is not the best one for communicating with contemporary political revolutionaries, who stress political liberation by any means necessary; that a 'new' black theological language is needed if black religion is going to articulate today the historical struggles of black people in America and the Third World. The question nevertheless remains: How was it possible for black people to endure the mental and physical stresses of slavery and still keep their humanity intact? I think the answer is found in black eschatology. Maybe what is needed is not a dismissal of the idea of heaven but a rein-terpretation of it, so that oppressed blacks today can develop styles of resistance not unlike those of their ancestors.

1. HEAVEN AND BLACK EXISTENCE

The place to begin is with Miles Fisher's contention that the spirituals are primarily 'historical documents'. They tell us about the black movement for historical liberation, the attempt of black people to define their present history in the light of their promised future and not according to their past miseries. Fisher notes that heaven for early black slaves referred not only to a transcendent reality beyond time and space; it designated the earthly places that blacks regarded as lands of freedom. Heaven referred to Africa, Canada, and the northern United States.[1]

Frederick Douglass wrote about the double meanings of these songs: 'We were at times remarkably buoyant, singing hymns, and making joyous exclamations, almost as triumphant in their tone as if we had reached a land of freedom and safety. A keen observer might have detected in our repeated singing of

O Canaan, sweet Canaan,
I am bound for the land of Canaan,

something more than a hope of reaching heaven. We meant to reach the *North*, and the *North* was our Canaan.'[2] Harriet Tubman also used the spirituals in her struggle to free black people from the bonds of slavery. The spirituals were communicative devices about the possibilities of earthly freedom. Sarah Bradford[3] reported how Tubman used the song in order to let her relatives and friends know that she intended to escape North to freedom.

When dat ar ole chariot comes,
    I'm gwine to lebe you,
I'm boun' for de promised land,
    Frien's, I'm gwine to lebe you.
I'm sorry, frien's, to lebe you,
    Farewell! oh, farewell!
But I'll meet you in de mornin'.
    Farewell! oh, farewell!
I'll meet you in de mornin',
    When you reach de promised land;
On de oder side of Jordan,
    For I'm boun' for de promised land.

As with Douglass, Tubman's concept of 'de promised land on de oder side of Jordan' was not just a transcendent reality. It was the North and later Canada. Said Harriet, after reaching free territory: 'I looked at my hands to see if I was de same person now I was free. Dere was such a glory ober everything, de sun came like gold trou de trees, and ober de fields, and I felt like I was in heaven.'[4]

However, she was not content to be free while others remained in bondage: 'I had crossed de line of which I had so long been dreaming. I was free; but dere was no one to welcome me to de land of freedom, I was a stranger in a strange land, and my home after all was down in de old cabin quarter, wid de ole folks, and my brudders and sisters. But to dis solemn resolution I came; I was free, and dey should be free also; I would make a home for dem in de North, and de Lord helping me, I would bring dem all dere. Oh, how I prayed den, lying all alone on de cold, damp ground; "Oh, dear Lord," I said, "I hain't got no friend but you. Come to my help, Lord, for I'm in trouble!" '[5] According to Sarah Bradford, Harriet went back south nineteen times and brought with her 'over three hundred pieces of living and breathing "property" '[6] to the promised land.

In this context 'Swing Low, Sweet Chariot' referred to the 'idea of escape by "chariot", that is, by means which a company could employ to proceed northward'. When black slaves sang, 'I looked over Jordan and what did I see, Coming for to carry me home', they were looking over the Ohio River. 'The band of angels' was Harriet or another conductor coming for him; and 'home' was a haven in the free states or Canada.[7] 'Steal away' meant to sneak into the woods for a secret slave meeting, and 'Follow the Drinking Gourd' meant following the Great Dipper to the Ohio River and freedom.[8]

But while it is true that heaven had its this-worldly topographical referents, not all black slaves could hope to make it to Africa, Canada, or even to the northern section of the United States. The ambiguity and failure of the American Colonization Society's experiments crushed the hopes of many black slaves who wanted to return to their African homeland. And blacks also began to realise that the North was not so significantly different from the South as they had envisioned, particularly in view of the Fugitive Slave Act of 1850 and the Dred Scott Decision in 1858. Black slaves began to realise that their historical freedom could not be assured as long as white racists controlled the governmental process of America. Thus they found it necessary to develop a style of freedom that *included* but *did not depend* upon historical possibilities. What could freedom mean for black slaves who could never expect to participate in the determination of the laws governing their lives? Must they continue to define freedom in terms of the possibility of escape and insurrection as if their humanity depended on their willingness to commit suicide? It was in response to this situation that the black concept of heaven developed.

For black slaves, who were condemned to carve out their existence in captivity, heaven meant that the eternal God had made a decision about their humanity that could not be destroyed by white slavemasters. Whites could drive them, beat them, and even kill them; but they believed that God nevertheless had chosen black slaves as his own and that this election bestowed upon them a freedom to be, which could not be measured by what oppressors could do to the physical body. Whites may suppress black history and define Africans as savages, but the words of slave-masters do not have to be taken seriously when the oppressed know that they have a somebodiness that is guaranteed by the heavenly Father who alone is the ultimate sovereign of the universe. This is what heaven meant for black slaves.

The idea of heaven provided ways for black people to affirm their humanity when other people were attempting to define them as non-persons. It enabled blacks to say yes to their right to be free by affirming God's promise to the oppressed of the freedom to be. That was what they meant when they sang about a 'city called heaven".

> I am a poor pilgrim of sorrow.
> I'm in this world alone.
> No hope in this world for tomorrow.
> I'm trying to make heaven my home.
> Sometimes I am tossed and driven.
> Sometimes I don't know where to roam.
> I've heard of a city called heaven.
> I've started to make it my home.

In the midst of economic and political disfranchisement, black slaves held themselves together and did not lose their spiritual composure, because they believed that their worth transcended governmental decisions. That was why they looked forward to 'walking in Jerusalem just like John' and longed for the 'camp meeting in the promised land'.

It is evident that the pre-scientific images of heaven in these songs point to a biblical emphasis usually glossed over by biblical scholars. Black slaves are expressing the Christian contention that the death and resur-rection of Christ bestows upon people a freedom that cannot be taken away by oppressors. They were saying: 'We are human beings and not even white slavemasters can do anything about that!'

2. THE TRANSCENDENT PRESENT

Even when there is no overt or hidden reference to specific historical events, the spirituals employ eschatological language to express trans-cendence in the slaves' present existence. 'I've *started* to make heaven my home', 'Marching up the heavenly road, I'm bound to fight till I die'— such lines make clear that black slaves were not passively waiting for the future; they were actively living as if the future were already present in their community.

O glory, glory, hallelujah!
  O glory, glory to that Lamb;
O glory, glory, hallelujah!
  Child of God, that's what I am!

To be a child of God had present implications. It meant that God's future had broken into the slave's historical present, revealing that God had defeated evil in Jesus' crucifixion and resurrection. The black slave could experience *now* a foretaste of that freedom which is to be fully revealed in the future. That was what the writer of I John had in mind when he wrote: 'We are God's children now' (3:2). The future had become present in the resurrection of Jesus and no one had to be a slave anymore. A slave's personhood or 'soul' was free to be what was consistent with God's act of liberation.

One day, one day, while walkin' along,
  Jesus done bless my soul;
I heard a voice an' saw no one,
  Jesus done bless my soul.
O go an' tell it on de mountain,
  Jesus done bless my soul;
O go an' tell it in de valley,
  Jesus done bless my soul.

Again, in a similar fashion, the slave described the realised dimensions of God's eschatological presence.

One day when I was walkin' along, Oh yes, Lord,
De element opened, an' de Love cam down, Oh yes, Lord,
I never shall forget dat day, Oh yes, Lord,
When Jesus washed my sins away, Oh yes, Lord.

These songs make clear that the future is not simply a reality to come. It is a reality that has already happened in Jesus' resurrection, and present now in the midst of the black struggle for liberation. To accept the future of God as disclosed in the present means that we cannot be content with present political order. God's eschatological presence makes for dis-contentment and renders the present subject to radical change. That was why black slaves could not 'sit down'. They were on the move, 'tryin' to get home'. The accepted the consequences of the eschatological King-dom, and opened their minds and hearts to the movement of the future. They were bound for the Kingdom that was breaking into the already new present, and they affirmed their willingness to 'git on board' that 'gospel train'.

Git on board, little chillen,
Git on board, little chillen,
Git on board, little chillen,
Dere's room for many a mo'.
De gospel trains a-comin',
I hear it jus' at han',
I hear de car wheels movin',
An' rumblin' thro de lan'.
De fare is cheap, an' all can go,
De rich an' poor are dere,
No second class a-board dis train,
No difference in de fare.

The only requirement for acceptance on the 'gospel train' was the willingness to *move*, to step into the future. Those who were bound to the present by earthly possessions would not likely give up everything and accept the risk of the future. But black slaves did not have that problem since their present meant only slavery. The could 'step on board' because they had nothing to lose and everything to gain. The 'gospel train' meant the possibility of freedom.

Because black slaves believed that the gospel was a message about the future of God, breaking into the reality of their present, they were liberated *from* the bondage of the present and free to be *for* God's future. In this sense, the partly revealed future of God, as disclosed in the cross and resurrection of Christ, made black people resist the condition of enslavement. Indeed, if the Kingdom was truly present in their midst, and if it was really ultimate, then they *had* to disobey all values that hindered their obedience to the coming Kingdom. Heaven then did not mean passivity but revolution against the present order. Against overwhelming odds, black people fought the structures of slavery and affirmed their membership in a 'city whose builder and maker was God'.

In the black spirituals, the image of heaven served functionally to liberate the black mind from the existing values of white society, enabling black slaves to think their own thoughts and do their own things. For Tubman and Douglass, heaven meant the risk of escape to the North and Canada; for Nat Turner, it was a vision from above that broke into the minds of believers, giving them the courage and the power to take up arms against slavemasters and mistresses. And for others, heaven was a perspective on the present, a spiritual, a song about 'another world . . . not made with hands'. It was a black life-style, a movement and a beat to the rhythm of freedom in the souls and bodies of black slaves. It was a hum, a moan, and a hope for freedom. Through song blacks were able to transcend the enslavement of the present and to live as if the future had already come.

Hope in the black spirituals is not a denial of history. Black hope accepts history, but believes that the historical is in motion, moving toward a divine fulfilment. It is the belief that things can be radically otherwise than they are: that reality is not fixed, but is moving in the direction of human liberation.

There is a balm in Gilead,
To make the spirit whole.
There is a balm in Gilead,
To heal the sin-sick soul.

To believe that there was hope in the midst of oppression meant that black slaves' vision of the future was not limited to their present state of slavery. They looked beyond the condition of servitude and perceived that the real meaning of their existence was still to come. The absurd present was not eternal, and they were free to change it according to their vision of the future. As Howard Thurman put it: 'It is an optimism that uses the pessimism of life as raw material out of which it creates its own strength.'[9]

The present moment of slavery was thus transcended by faith in God's future, a liberated future. The divine future broke into their wretchedness. The seized his future, the Word of his promise, as the strength for carving out a future for themselves. They had also to seize the future from white masters and overlords who were continuing to deny them any future other than that of chattel to be sold on the auction block in slave marts.

To create the future in the 'extreme situation' of American slavery was very difficult for black slaves. It meant accepting the burden and the risk of the 'not yet'. Actually, when they encountered the divine presence and promise, as revealed in the event of Jesus' death and resurrection, they knew that there was only *one* possibility for authentic human existence. And that was to *live* in *freedom* for the *future*. They said what they said and did what they did not because of any 'logic' in the physical reality that encompassed them—where could they find an empowering logic in the situation of their servitude?—but because they intuitively understood the necessity to affirm life, to respond to life. In this sense they did not 'choose' their future; it was thrust upon them as the only divine possibility reconcilable with their humanity. This all-important affirmation rested not in an epistemological base, but on an ontological base that allowed them no other response.

3. THE TRANSCENDENT FUTURE

The concept of heaven was not exhausted by historical reality or present existence. It expressed something besides the capacity of black people to be human in the midst of suffering and despair. In the spirituals, heaven was also hope in the future of God, an expectation that the contradictions of slavery were not ultimate. They believed that life did not end with death and that somewhere in the 'bosom' of God's eternity, He would rectify the wrongs against His people. 'We are God's children now; it does not yet appear what we shall be, *but we know that when he appears we shall be like him, for we shall see him as he is*' (I John 3:2). The 'not yet' affirmed the *novum* of divine presence that was still to come. It was the expectation of the future of God, grounded in the resurrection of Jesus, that was the central theological focus of the black religious experience. This hope in a radically new future, defined solely by God the Liberator, was expressed in the spirituals in two ways:

(1) language about heaven as a different sort of *place* after death; and
(2) language about the 'last days', a new kind of *time*.

1.   Heaven was a place where the oppressed would 'lay down dat heavy load' as mother and father had done before. It was a place where slaves would put on their robes, take up their harps, and put on their shoes and wings. It was 'dat Rock', the slaves' true home, the Promised Land down by the riverside. 'In dat great gettin' up mornin', the oppressed of the land would be received into a 'New Jerusalem'.

I want to go to heaven when I die,
To shout salvation as I fly.
When I get to heaven goin' set right down,
Gwin-er ask my Lord for starry crown.
Now wait till I gits my gospel shoes,
Gwin-er walk 'bout heaven an' carry de news.

Heaven was the place for the mourner, the despised, rejected and black.

My Lord! Po' mourner's got a home at las'.
Mourner's got a home at las'.
O, No harm, Lord, no harm,

Go tell brudder Elijah,
No harm, Lord, No harm,
Po' mourner's got a home at las'.

It was a home indeed, where slaves would sit down by Jesus, eat at the welcome table, sing and shout, because there would be nobody there to turn them out. The black slave took seriously Jesus' promise in the Fourth Gospel that he would prepare a place for them, a place with many mansions (14:23).

In bright mansions above,
In bright mansions above,
Lord, I want to live up yonder;
In bright mansions above.

The 'mansions above' were God's Kingdom, a heavenly place of rest and peace from the pain of slavery.

No more hard trial in de kingdom; no more tribulation, no more
    parting, no more quarreling, back-biting in de kingdom,
No more sunshine fer to bu'n you; no more rain fer to wet you.
Every day will be Sunday in heaven.

Heaven was God's eschatological promise; it was a place of 'golden streets', 'pearly gates', and 'the long white robes'. There would be no more sadness, no more sorrow and no more hunger—for everybody is 'goin' feast off'n milk an' honey'.

2. Black slaves also expressed their anticipation of God's new future with apocalyptic imagination. 'Where shall I be when the first trumpet soun'; soun' so loud till it woke up de dead?' 'One day, one day 'bout twelve o'clock, O this ol' earth goin' reel an' rock.' 'O My Lord, what a morning, when the stars begin to fall!' 'When the sun refuse to shine, when the moon goes down in blood!' 'In dat great getting up morning', 'de world will be on fire', and 'you'll see de stars a-fallin', de forked lightning, de coffins bursting', and 'de righteous marching'. 'The dumb will talk, the lame will walk, the blind will see, and the deaf will hear.'

These songs emphasised the inability of the present to contain the reality of the divine future. In this sense the spirituals were 'other-worldly'. They stressed the utter distinction between the present and the future. The hope of black slaves was not of this world, not in the 'hell of a completely understood humanity'.[10] They hoped for 'the One who is never knowable, who, in the constant revolution and "transformation" within faith, is alone disclosed as a promise'.[11] It was a hope against the hopes of this world; against the self-erected gods of finite men. It was hope for the God of the Exodus, of the prophets, and of the resurrected Christ, whose will is known through the promise disclosed in his liberating activity in history. And it is through the strength of their hope in God that the oppressed are saved (Romans 8:24).

It was this transcendent element of hope (as expressed in black music) which elevated black people above the limitations of the slave experience, and enabled them to view black humanity independently of their oppressors. Through music black slaves ritualised their existence and gave to their lives a dimension of promise and new reality that could not be contained in human theologies and philosophies. As they accepted the promise and took it to themselves, it became a real force in their history; hence 'a new dimension of promise and new reality'. The concept of heaven in black music placed the people in a 'New Earth' and transformed their perceptions of black existence from the nothingness of the present condition of slavery into being-for-the-future. Heaven was a vision of a new Black Humanity.

Some critics will observe that even if black eschatology is interpreted as something other than a description of the goegraphy of the next world, it still introduces a jarringly non-historical element into the analysis of liberation. It speaks of an ultimate liberation that is primarily of God and not of people, of the next world and not this world. If authentic liberation is an *historical* reality (having to do with economics, politics and the sociality of human existence), how can it be reconciled with 'A-settin' down with Jesus, Eatin' honey and drinkin' wine, Marchin' round de throne, Wid Peter, James, and John'? What possible relationship could the 'gospel feast' have with the politics of Black Power, or the Marxist's claim that liberation is a historical determination of which the human being is sole agent? As Gajo Petrovic, interpreting Marx, put it: '*The question of the essence of freedom*, like the question of the essence of man, *is not only a question*. It is *at once participation in production of freedom*. It is an activity through which freedom frees itself.'[12] Is not heaven an opium, a clever religious trick devised by oppressors so that the oppressed will not challenge their rule on earth? True, white oppressors did preach 'pie in the sky' as a means to get black people to accept their exploitation. But oppressors have over the years also used distorted versions of Democracy, Marxism, and even Black Power as their means to confuse and control the oppressed, and they will distort any world-view to camouflage their own interests.

Accordingly, the problems of black religion today will not be solved by rejecting it outright simply because white people have misused black religion for their own selfish interests. The task, however, of black theologians is to move beyond the distortions of black religion to the authentic substance of black religious experience so that it can continue to serve as a positive force in liberating black people. And black theologians will find that the strongest counterweight to the obstacles in the way of historical liberation is that vision of the future defined by the oppressed black slaves. As Walter Benjamin has observed: 'It is only for the sake of those without hope that hope is given for us.'[13]

Behind the apocalyptic vision of powerless black slaves there was precisely this openness to the future which moved them beyond their finite capabilities. From the midst of their very enslavement they looked *forward* to the time of deliverance when they would leave the unbearable oppression of the world around them. To them this looking forward was no mere role assigned to them in an apocalyptic myth; it was an authentic account of what they were experiencing and struggling with as slaves. Black slaves believed that when people become submissive because they are afraid of the future, God remains the absolute future and continues his work of liberation even though people are passive and inactive. When the people of Israel complained to Moses about the approaching Egyptian army, preferring the fleshpots of Egypt to the uncertainty of the future, Yahweh said: 'Tell the people of Israel to go *forward*' (Exodus 14:15). Authentic human liberation is found only in the struggle for the future that is grounded in divine liberation. The 'divine element' stands for that reality in human encounter which will not let people remain content with slavery, injustice and oppression.

Notes

1. Miles Mark Fisher *Negro Slave Songs in the United States* (New York 1953).

2. *Life and Times of Frederick Douglass* (New York 1962) p. 159. A reprint of the 1892 revised edition.

3. Sarah Bradford *Harriet Tubman: The Moses of Her People* (New York 1961) p. 27-28). A reprint of the second edition of 1886.

4. *Ibid.* p. 30.

5. *Ibid.* p. 31-32.

6. *Ibid.* p. 33.

7. Earl Conrad *Harriet Tubman* (New York 1969) p. 77.

8. *Ibid.* p. 78 from Richard Randall 'Fighting Sons of the Unemployed' *The Sunday Worker Progressive Weekly* 3 September 1939, p. 2.

9. Howard Thurnam *Deep River* (New York 1969) p. 56. Originally published in 1945.

10. Johannes B. Metz 'God Before Us Instead of Theological Arguments' in *Cross Current* 18 No. 3 (Summer 1968).

11. *Ibid.*

12. *Marx in the Mid-Twentieth Century* (New York 1967) p. 120. Italics in original.

13. Cited in Herbert Marcuse *One-Dimensional Man* (Boston 1964) p. 257.

Juan Luis Ruiz de la Peña

The Element of Projection and Belief in Heaven

FEUERBACH ends the first part of his *The Essence of Christianity* with a chapter expressedly devoted to demonstrating that the heaven of Christian belief is a projection.[1] Following him, Marxist and Freudian criticisms of religion repeat the charge. This thesis is obviously not put forward as a neutral observation, but is designed to prove the invalidity of religious thinking in general and Christian thinking in particular. 'Projection' is used in the sense of 'mystification': the projective nature of teaching on heaven reveals its illusory character, thereby confirming the objective falseness of religious imagery.

The first part of this study tries to show how far the eternal life we profess to believe in in the Creed is a *Wunschbild*, a wish-image of everything man continually longs and hopes for. But the basic question remains unanswered by the conclusions of this first part: it is by no means clear that thought involving projective elements is *eo ipso* necessarily false. We need to ask whether (and to what extent) the 'projection-mystification' equation is reasonably acceptable. Once this central point has been examined, we can then move on to evaluating the positive or negative role played by projective elements in deciding the plausibility of Christian belief in heaven.

1. HEAVEN AS A PROJECTION

Christianity is, essentially, a soteriology, the good news of salvation. This, in turn, in the final analysis, is seen as an eschatological dimension. 'Heaven' is just the term given to this eschatological phase of the process

72

of salvation. How do we define the content and essential characteristics of fully saved existence?

(a) Life

Man, who regards himself as an absolute value, seeks first stability in his being, the affirmation and consolidation of his existence. So death is seen as the ultimate evil. The *logos* about death feeds on the inextinguishable protest which its fatal necessity produces in the human mind. No offer of salvation or programme for the future can be convincing if it fails to take account of the mortal condition of those to whom it is directed. More than that: if the offer of salvation fails to find a way out of human mortality, it becomes abstract and disappointing, because what, then, does its salvation affect? The world, history, humanity, but not the particular singular individual? This way leads soteriology to pure and simple abstraction; by giving the universal primacy over the particular, it confers a fictitious hypostasis on the former to disguise the brutally wounding fact that *there is no salvation* for the latter.

The concept of irrefutable mortality takes on scandalous dimensions in the framework of humanist anthropologies. The assignment of absolute value to man, in the ontological as well as in the axiological order, is faced with its hardest test in the form of the threat of total extinction. The death of an absolute value, in the sense of its no-longer-being, is an absolute tragedy, and sheds the suspicion of senselessness on the rest of surviving reality.

In the Christian faith, each and every individual is not only a member of a species, but a person, an absolutely valid entity and as such supremely worthy of salvation. The reality arising from the Creator's design enjoys an intelligibility that cannot be reduced to the *absurdum* into which it would be plunged if the total loss of him who rules and presides over it as 'the image of God' were the *ultima ratio* of historical existence. Therefore, the prime content of the Christian idea of salvation is life. Life despite death, or rather: death as transit and not death as terminus; this is what gives Christianity the possible condition for discourse on salvation. The only possible condition: without this, any other soteriological content is subject to the corrosive power of decay, which contradicts its finest purpose, or risks falling into a vacuum through failing to find a concrete subject in which it can become incarnate, make itself genuinely real.

(b) Interpersonal love

On of the most firmly rooted intuitions in the human heart is that of the unconquerable power of love. From the Diotima of Plato's *Symposium* to Arnaud Chartrain in Marcel's *La soif* or Marie in Ionesco's *Le roi se meurt*, through the poetry of the Song of Songs and the troubadours, there runs that presage of love conquering all, stronger even than death, such as we all desire, 'Loving someone means saying to him: "You will not die"' (Marcel); 'If you love with folly, if you love absolutely, death recedes' (Ionesco).

It was this same universal intuition that set the biblical authors on the trail of a life that would conquer seemingly-victorious death. Psalms 16, 49 and 73, Paul's 'being-with-Christ', John's 'remaining in love', and many more, are examples of biblical variations on the theme *love-is-stronger-than-death*. If all love promises eternity, God's love has not merely to promise it, but to grant it, since he holds life and death in his hand. The Christian concept of the alternative of death and immortality is fully resolved in the course of the loving dialogue between God and man, that is, in the sphere of human history. In the various rationalist formulations of this alternative, immortality would derive from nature, not from history. In Scripture, on the other hand, the logic of love is the only one capable of explaining the origin of life in its total gratuitousness, by simultaneously proposing the—equally unique and gratuitous—guarantee of life after death. Basing its hope on a post-mortal existence in this manner, Christian faith appropriates the postulate of the secular poetical-philosophical tradition that discovers secret affinities in the *Thánatos-Eros* dyad.

So the death of the individual challenges the love of God and tests the identity of both man (is he an absolute value?) and God (is God love?). The response to the challenge corroborates the immortality glimpsed in any life born from and for love.

(c) Vision of God, Divinisation of Man

The affirmation of survival after death, far from removing the problematic character of the human condition, intensifies it. In effect: death is one dimension of contingency, certainly the most obvious and drastic, *but not the only one*. The abolition of the temporal limit, but of no other, poses more problems than it solves; it is like a chronic endorsement of all other limitations. Simone de Beauvoir's novel *Tous les hommes sont mortels* is a strikingly effective illustration of the tragedy of an existence condemned to temporal immortality, in which there is no longer any stimulus, any ultimate goal, where everything is suffused with the boredom of unreason, the tedious temporality of the indefinitely revocable.

If immortality is to be salvation rather than perdition, it must bring, besides a prolongation of the life span, a promotion of the individual to an ontologically qualitatively higher status. The surpassing of contingency cannot be a purely regional phenomenon; if it were, it would have to make good the global deficit of being painfully imprisoned in each of the manifestations of the self. This is why the '*eritis sicut dei*', the Promethean temptation, is the classic temptation; its recurrent emergence in the history of different anthropologies bears witness to the fact that it represents one of the ineradicable tendencies of human nature.

The Christian faith sees heaven as the goal of the process of divinisation implanted in time by grace. The term 'seeing God', often taken in a dry intellectualist sense, has a much denser and more complex meaning in the New Testament. In an Eastern court, the king is inaccessible to the majority of his subjects; only the courtiers are allowed to see him as he is. Seeing the king is placed in the context of living close by him. So, analogously, seeing God means sitting at his table, enjoying his closeness, sharing his life, becoming part of his being. '. . . we shall be like him because we shall see him as he really is' (1 Jn 3:2). Seeing engenders likeness; eternal life is becoming divine.

(d) Belonging to Society and the World

The call to a truly universal solidarity, embracing all men of all times, even as unrealisable ideal, lies at the heart of all humanist socio-juridical systems. Likewise, man's unlimited dominion over the cosmos is the ideal unflaggingly pursued by technology—from the lowest to the highest forms—and art. Artistic creation undeniably represents the highest peak of man's transformation of brute matter into domesticated and humanised artefact. The epic grandeur of the victory of *logos* over cosmos finds its most expressive parable in the tractability of marble to the sculptor's chisel. But there are disheartening aspects of this *logos-cosmos* dialectic: science itself, which has set man up as lord of his planet, tells him that this is only a peripheral speck in the vastness of the universe. Every technological advance is a paradoxical conquest of a small strip of reality at the price of discovering new tracts of *terra incognita* beyond the area dominated.

The heaven of Christian belief is not discouraged by these breaks in the progress of society and the world. Eternal life, communion in the being of God, will also be a communion of saints, the achievement of a solidarity without boundaries of time and space, the bringing of the dream of universal brotherhood to fruition, where we shall know the truth—now only glimpsed darkly through the eyes of faith—that we are all brothers of one another. Furthermore, consummated humanity will see its dominion over the world finally established. The new creation is the *topos* connatural to this humanity, open to a creative power for which work will be leisure and leisure work, in such a way that action, always gratifying, will impress the shape of the human spirit on the cosmos.

These four are the principal contents of the articulation of Christian doctrine concerning heaven. The careful reader will have noticed that the foregoing has been expressed, in a way, tendentiously: far from trying to hide from the suspicion of projection which is our starting-point, the projective character of the contents discussed has been emphasised.[2] This projective character is even more clearly evident in the images and symbols in which these contents are usually clothed, so there is no need to dwell further on this aspect of the matter.

If one wanted to comment on Feuerbach's view of the Christian heaven, one might criticise him for failing to appreciate the full dimension of the phenomenon of projection in relation to it. In effect, his view of heaven is tinged with spiritualism and individualism, evidently because this was the only view suggested by the theology of his time. The title of his chapter establishes the link between 'the Christian heaven' and 'personal immortality'. But leaving this comment aside, and within its limits, his thesis that heaven represents the object of man's desire to become like God, and therefore a theomorphic cloak for anthropology, in which the human being transcends his constitutive contingency by sublimating it, is a valid one. As he notes in *The Essence of Christianity,* revelation speaks of eternal life in terms of 'wish-fulfilment'; its 'beyond' is coined on the basis of 'the here-and-now freed from what appears as limitation, as evil'; 'the content of the beyond is the eternal happiness of the personality existing here below with the limitations and obstacles imposed by nature'.

But, as has been pointed out above, Feuerbach did not stop at this observation. His thesis of heaven as projection is joined by another, this time involving a value judgment: the Christian heaven is *mere* projection; the projective nature of this representation is incompatible with its objective reality; eternal life exists only in the minds of those who foolishly let themselves be fascinated by the miracles of the imagination.

2. PROJECTION: SOURCE OF MYSTIFICATION OR FORGE OF UTOPIA?

The question that immediately arises is this: How far can the projective element be acquitted of the sin of mystification? Is it true that projection is always alien to the logic of rational discourse, and therefore incompatible with an objective reading of reality? This is the marrow of Feuerbach's objection to the doctrine of eternal life.

Quoting Bloch has become a theological *trope* comparable to the earlier vogue for quoting Thomas Aquinas. But there are few theological problems more closely related to the debt I now acknowledge to the author of *Das Prinzip Hoffnung.* No one has tackled the question of the value of thought nourished by projective elements more lucidly. In view of the new orientations provided by his work, there is no alternative but to turn to him.

For a start, Bloch is equally acerbic with both Freud and Feuerbach, the two masters of anti-projective suspicion. Freud has the undeniable merit of having shown that psychic activity cannot be held to coincide simply with conscious activity, and of having studied the functions of the unconscious and its incidence on human behaviour with unparalleled expertise. But, so Bloch alleges, he fails to take account of the most decisive dimension of consciousness: that by which the ego reaches out to the future, that which incubates and feeds the optative potential of the affects of expectation. Freud, in a word, leaves out the *pre-conscious* in the sense of 'still-not-conscious'.[3]

As for Feuerbach, Bloch accuses him of neglecting the time factor in his philosophy, which leads him to a notion of man circumscribed by an unchanging *ousía* or by the current face of humanity: what is lacking here, Bloch claims, is the infinity of the unfinished. So his thesis of the divine as hypostasis of the human does not stand up; for it to be valid, it would have to postulate a *homo absconditus* corresponding to the *Deus absconditus* of the medieval Schoolmen and Pascal. The vacuum created by the denial of God would have to be filled with the processually emergent reality of this *homo absconditus* (PH, pp. 1517 ff, 1529; cf. pp. 1405 ff). Feuerbach's materialism is still a contemplative one, crippled by his adoration of the simply given and by his mechanistic interpretation (pp. 297 ff). Rejecting all transcendence as alienating, on the grounds that it comes from imagination and desires, he fails to see that he is guilty, in his turn, of another gross mystification: making the human species in the abstract an abstraction inherent in the individual (p. 304 f). The only thing capable of freeing him from this abstraction would be consideration of the future, and this he has not managed because the *actum* makes him forget the *fieri,* and the *fixum* left by history in its wake hides the open space before him (p. 328 f).

Bloch, in short, attacks Freud and Feuerbach for the archeological character of their respective points of view. His, on the other hand, is going to be an eschatological mode of thought, whose embryonic cell is 'the not-yet' and whose principal categories will be: possibility, process, daydream, *Novum,* utopia and hope.

Reality is matter; matter is possibility. History is a process of bringing this possibility to fruition. An interpretation of reality restricted to pure observation of brute facts, shackled by cataloguing established data, is hardly realistic, since reality itself has not taken its final shape. 'The process is still undetermined. . . . The essence has not yet been unveiled' (PH, p. 223). 'The world is full of disposition to something, of tendency toward something, of latency with something, and this *something* toward which the world is tending is the outcome of intention' (p. 17). Since reality is for the moment in exile, in its pre-history, the true ontology is one based not on the classical principle of identity ($A = A$), but on $A = not\text{-}yet\ A$; the present predicate is not yet the final form of the subject (p. 361).

This ontology of the *not-yet* is matched by a psychology of the same type. Man, the agent of process, is in process himself. The depths of an individual contain a 'pressure' (*Drang*) impelling him forward, evidenced in an undefined 'tension' (*Streben*) which is exteriorised in the form of 'aspiration' (*Sehnen*). When this has an object, it becomes 'quest' (*Suchen*), working through 'drive' (*Trieb*) and capable of representing its goal to itself in advance in the form of 'wish-image' (*Wunschbild*). Drives, finally, take shape in 'affects' (*Affekten*), among which 'affects of expectation' (*Erwartungs-Affekte*) stand out, the first of which, as we shall see, reaches for hope (pp. 49 ff).

This scheme of human psychology responds, as will have been observed, to what was earlier singled out as the privileged dimension of consciousness: the pre-conscious or *not-yet-conscious*. The true pre-conscious is the workshop in which novelty is elaborated, the 'twilight to the future', 'the psychic portrayal of the not-yet-become' (p. 143). The not-yet conscious is revealed to us in daydreams (*Tagträume*). Man, in fact, does not dream only when asleep; night dreamsn clearly regressiven should give way to the dream of the waking imagination, whose natural tendency is anticipation. The pre-appearance which shows us concerns real possibility, since it is worked out in the unfolding of the personality and the world toward a horizon open to creativity. Day-dreams spread in extent and depth till they take on the dimensions of a Utopia (p. 105).

Utopia is the end term of the process of fulfilment of possibility, an end term espied by daydreams and their wish-images; it cannot be reduced to the purely given, since it represents an absolutley unheard-of *Novum*. Confidence in the epiphany of this *Novum,* not a simple restoration of the *primum* nor a mere evolutionary derivative from it, is what keeps the process in motion. Hope, therefore, is *the principle* in the Aristotelian sense of the term *arché*: the *basis* of every ontological and psychological reality, the support of the not-yet-become and the not-yet-conscious. It is, then, 'not only a fundamental property of the human consciousness; it is also a basic determinant of all objective reality' (p. 5).

On the basis of the hope principle, Bloch describes the ultimate future, the *Novum ultimum,* in terms reminiscent of biblical eschatology: 'a world without deceit', 'a happiness as yet unknown', 'heaven on earth', 'the world our home', 'a new earth', '*Summum Bonum*', etc. Even death will have been overcome ('taken up into victory'): the *homo absconditus* who finally emerges will be 'extra-territorial' to the 'final enemy' and will usher in an original manner of permanence of being, immune to the decay inherent in process, which will be abolished with the abolition of process itself (pp. 1389 ff). Wish-images will in the end reach their objective, thereby justifying their validity and their ability to lead the world from the state it is in today to its end, when the real genesis of reality will take place. Daydreams, far from being fallacious and evasive mystifications, are the tools for the transformation of the world as it is (a theatre of contradictions) into the world as it should and will be (a homeland of identity).[4]

The vigorous revindication of the projective element implicit in Bloch's interpretation of reality can also, *mutatis mutandis,* be found in other independent Marxist thinkers.[5] This is worth bearing in mind when answering the question: Despite all the objections, why should the believer not cease to give his hope shape in projective structures? Because he is Christian, or because he is human? This apparently reductionist question is imposed by the fact that, while Christians have their Divine Comedy, Marxists have their Concrete Utopia. Without one or the other, are we truly human? By which I mean: Is it humanly possible to live starved of the horizon opened up by the projective function? Is the present, *tout court,* habitable without life breaking down into the vegetative atomism of 'eat, drink and be merry'?

3. FINAL CONSIDERATIONS

The aim of this article is not to attempt an 'apologetic for heaven'. Apart from the basic difficulty of such an undertaking (which is also questionable from the viewpoint of the Christian faith), such an apologetic would not differ greatly from that provided by an apologetic for God or religion in general, which would reduce the specific value of this essay. Its aim is rather to show that the projective element, which helps shape our view of eternal life, is not something the Christian has to be ashamed of. The fact is that any *project* suggestive of the future—and what use is any project that is not at least suggestive?—contains an inescapable dose of *projection*: etymology is highly revealing here, as in so many other cases. Therefore, either man renounces the faculty of projecting, which would be tantamount to renouncing the future, or he openly accepts the charge of projection contained in the meaning of the word 'project' itself. As we have seen, the use of the projective element is not confined to Christian eschatological belief; it also appears in secular attempts to delimit and forecast the future which take its open nature seriously and therefore quarrel with the various sorts of determinism that encapsulate it in supposedly unsurpassable limitations.

The genuinely human future spans two elements: the element of *novelty,* in which its power of fascination resides, and by which it offers a mode of being qualitatively superior to our present one, and the element of *continuity,* without which this future would be alien and extraneous to the present, which would then not feel drawn towards it nor attracted by its mystery. This second element alone justifies projection; more, it requires it, if our prospecting of the future is to speak an intelligible language and if this future is to be perceptible as a promise made to the present. A systematic veto on projection imprisons the goal of the impulses, desires and aspirations of the human psyche in universal non-communication. This is why it is not justifiable to reject Christian teaching on eternal life on the grounds that it inverts or abolishes the contradictions of temporal life. Supposing that belief in heaven is not limited to the banishment of present contradictions (remember the warning phrase of 1 Col 2:7 ff: '. . . what the eye has not seen nor the ear heard . . .'), but also willingly assumes the unpredictability of God's communicative love (the source of the *novelty* element), it then seems obvious that the proclamation of the *eschaton* can be humanly pronounced and understood only if it starts from the present experience of a situation in need of salvation: hence the inevitability of the *continuity* element and, with it, the projective factor.

Furthermore, while safeguarding a minimum content of continuity between present and future, projection moves by hesitant approximations in the direction of a *Novum* hazily glimpsed but truly possible, and therefore not to be left out of account in an objective interpretation of reality. An *a priori* prohibition of all projection produces a real short-circuit in the choice mechanism lodged in the anticipatory consciousness so wisely described by Bloch; it ties the future to sterile reiteration of the past and the present, immunising these against novelty, which is to say *against salvation*.

To sum up: what is at stake in the debate on the validity of projection is the type of world-view from which one starts. If the *Weltanschauung* is one restricted to positivist statement of naked facticity, one that removes the notes of possibility and process from the sphere of the real, then the projective function has to be repressed. The pejorative connotations attaching to the term 'projection' derive from this mentality. A closed ontology, seeing reality as a *fixum,* or at best an evolutionary unfolding of what can germinate from the present configuration of reality, will see projection as a mystification. Its future will be either pure continuation of the present or the *Brave New World* of Huxley's ferocious satire. An open ontology, on the other hand, ready to allow space for the *Novum* to grow in, is convinced that the present is a *state* of fermentation and genesis of the future—of something essentially different and better; it feels intuitively that tomorrow cannot be reduced to yesterday, either in daily profile, or in its quasi-biological development, which is organically necessary and can therefore be surely defined, foreseen and planned for. Within such a *Weltanschauung,* the correlative categories of *projection* and *utopia* are redeemed, without apology, from their earlier deprecatory estimation; judgment of the validity of their contents has then to proceed with other parameters, not including simple rejection of the projective element.[6]

The Christian has to profess his faith in eternal life in the knowledge that his conceptualisation of it includes projection; in the knowledge too that this is how one of the objects of man's most legitimate and inevitable impulses takes shape: the explanation of the present through hope-inspired utopic prophecy of the future. A future, furthermore, which—as Pannenberg reminded Bloch[7]—as *'regnum venturum'*, has to be 'ontologically founded on itself', if it is to be given more substance than that of a simple wish-image. All of which, naturally, does not exempt the believer (and more so the theologian) from the duty of refining and relativising his verbal expressions of the word of God. Of adopting, in the end, Paul's words already quoted: '. . . what the eye has not seen nor the ear heard . . .' as a critical and demythologising coefficient of his representations.

Translated by Paul Burns

Notes

1. L. Feuerbach 'The Christian heaven or personal immortality' in *The Essence of Christianity* (3rd ed. London 1893); *idem. Gedanken über Tod und Unsterblichkeit* (Stuttgart 1960).

2. The magisterium of the Church itself seems to admit the existence of this element of projection on at least one point. See GS 39a, where God is said to be preparing a new dwelling place, 'whose blessedness will answer and surpass all the longings for peace which spring up in the human heart'.

3. *Das Prinzip Hoffnung* (Frankfurt 1959) p. 131. (Subsequent references in the text).

4. Christian belief in becoming like God through the beatific vision also drew an appreciative comment from Bloch: 'the highest form of wish-image against death' (*PH*, p. 1331).

5. J. L. Ruiz de la Peña *Muerte y Marxismo humanista: Aproximación teológica* (Salamanca 1978) *passim*, esp. chs. II-V.

6. One of these parameters must of course be concerned with deciding the degree of plausibility attaching to projection. To say that not all projection is necessarily false is not to say that is necessarily true.

7. W. Pannenberg 'Der Gott der Hoffnung' in *Grundfragen systematischer Theologie* (Gottingen 1967) p. 387-98.

Christian Duquoc

Heaven on Earth?

EVEN Christians are becoming increasingly critical of received notions
of 'heaven'. Numerous believers, particularly among the educated, find
what the Churches professed or still profess about life after death imaginary and incredible or even pernicious. Inspired by Marxist or psychoanalytical systems of interpretation, they detect inadmissible interests
at work behind the nostalgic charm of the imagery: an infantile rejection
of the absolute nature of death and a far from selfless turning aside from
revolutionary commitments in the here and now. These Christians are
concerned to recover what was and still is alienated, and to affirm that if
there is indeed a 'heaven' it is to be found in this world in the blessings of
God: in human brotherhood and freedom as they are experienced and
developed.

The aversion of many Christians to the idea of a 'heaven' after death
parallels the active recovery by secular movements and ideologies of
promises that have hitherto been religious. Revolutionary projects, forms
of belief in the immanent progressiveness of science and technology, and
various utopias won general acceptance with the onset of the industrial
age. Paradise was no longer inaccessible but became the possible fruit of
an actual transforming energy.

Traditional believers find something almost daemonic in the diversion
of their ultimate conviction into an active and effective will to create a
'heaven on earth'. In these Promethean movements they discern one of
the most dangerous forms of the typically modern apostasy: a realisation
of human happiness without the aid of God and independently of Christ's
liberating action. This assurance of a future in which mankind will
become free and fraternal by its own power seems to them laden with

sinister consequences which have found their unhappy signals in the history of our own times.

The summary account I have just given offers a typology of Christian behaviour divided into that which is animated by a simultaneously mythical and active image of 'heaven' and incarnates a will to enact the evangelical promise in the here-and-now, and that which finds perverse any negation of the beyond in favour of an illusion of an earthly paradise. This somewhat schematic typology of the two approaches serves to define one of the problems faced by theology today: whether completely to adopt the psychoanalytical and Marxist viewpoints in the hope of revealing a gospel truth divested of cultural images which deny it any present efficacy, or to allow a risk of reformism by articulating a traditional notion (in this case, a non-terrestrial heaven) in terms demands resulting from radical criticism.

As far as I am concerned, holding as I do that it is impossible to establish any *a priori* theory of social development, an historical perspective seems appropriate to the foregoing questions. I shall also try to show that initial Christian hope did not make a radical separation between 'heaven' and the 'here-and-now' of the kind received in present-day Christianity. I think that this separation was conditioned by the frustrated Chrisianisation of the Roman Empire, and the disappointment resulting from mediaeval Christianity. If this hypothesis is tenable, heaven as an inversion of the here-and-now would depend on the inability of the powers that be to ensure the existence of brotherhood, freedom and plenty as they have been promised. Hence it would be pointless to try to evaluate the idea of heaven offered by this historical derivation in the light of the New Testament. In fact, it is in the relation between this historical movement and the New Testament that the problem with which I am concerned—a heaven on earth?—might well be elucidated to some extent.

1. AN HISTORICAL DERIVATION: HEAVEN IN RETREAT

Former beliefs are coming into their own again: Jesus' promise cannot be shorn of its earthly reference. Jewish messianism at the time of the New Testament, in spite of its broad frame of reference, relied on a temporal interpretation of the Promise. It did not necessarily signify a will to power or political imperialism. The best spirits of Israel thought that the peace of God proclaimed by the Messiah would benefit everyone. The choice of the people of Israel operated in favour of a future in which all the nations of the world would be beneficiaries. Christians did not deny this conviction.

The Easter event did not oust but reinforced this assurance. There are traces in the New Testament of a fond hope that Christ would come again to re-establish the promised Kingdom (see the epistles to the Thessalonians). To be sure, as time passed impatient or querulous believers did come to doubt the strong bases of the promises (2 Pet. 3). Peter seeks to calm these fears; he invokes the patience of God, re-examines apocalyptical images, and reveals his conviction that the old world is nearly at an end and the new world is taking its place.

Millenarianism testifies still to the intensity of hope among the early Christians (Rev. 20); it was very successful until the Christianisation of the Empire in the fourth century. Irenaeus, in Book V of *Adversus haereses*,[1] uses elevated images to offer an earthly interpretation of the Promise. He finds it inconceivable that there should be no continuity between sharing in the divine happiness in the world beyond death and life on this earth. He also points out that the happy realm desired by God is inaugurated in the joy experienced in this world. He then describes in rich and magnificent terms the era of plenty, freedom and brotherhood which anticipates the untold joy which is still to come. The thousand years of Revelation 20 represents the period of time needed to become accustomed to happiness.

There were strong criticisms of millenarianism. Origen, and later Augustine,[2] condemned it for its gross materialism. Imaginative excesses in descriptions of the splendid orgies of the era of Christ's reign explain the violence of these accusations. But there is nothing to show that that is the reason for the decay of this conviction. Those condemnations did not finally dissolve what was to revive later in peripheral sects and movements. I would cite political factors as responsible for removing all credibility from the notion of a heaven inaugurated on earth, in a time beyond need and wretchedness, where everything would finally be permitted in innocence and brotherhood.

In fact, enthusiasm was so strong at the time of the conversion of Constantine that it was thought that the Christ-era had at last begun.[3] The mystic dream was both realised and refuted in the political realm. Once the Empire had become Christian and the Church was in a privileged position, there was nothing to prevent an already secular dream from becoming reality. In principle, the Kingdom had already arrived. The derisory nature of its realisation, the repeated setbacks, and the decadence that put paid to the Empire allowed more exclusivity to the notion of a unique heaven owing nothing to this world. Later versions of Christianity widened the gulf between the here-and-now and the beyond. The Inquisition was the reverse of the earthly paradise. Millenarianism had dreamed of brotherhood and plenty; the powers that be, devout as they were, found no other means than violence of confronting the true or imaginary resistance with which they were faced.

As against the hypothesis I have just proposed, one might object that millenarianism had not taken into account the delay of the Parousia: that is, it had not taken a true measure of the way in which the risen Christ was absent in virtue of his ascension, and that for that reason it depended on models contradicted by the novelty of the Gospel. Certainly millenarianism did not sufficiently assess the novelty of Christianity in relation to Jewish Messianism, but the expression in the imagery of dreams of a demand for non-separation between the here-and-now and the Kingdom of God is a healthy sign; millenarianism hoped for an earth ruled by justice and free from exploitation. It was no accident that later on, on the basis of a disappointment caused by Christianity, it became a revolutionary ferment. I am not forgetting that the memory of Christian millenarianism, because of resentment of the inadequate control of our history by the Church, strongly encouraged the gulf between the inaccessibility of the Promise and our earth. I would add, however, that this gulf would not have been so great without a social interplay of common interests between the privileged hierarchical Church and the dominant forces of the day. Millenarianist ideals were justly asserted in a minority Church that was often subject to persecution. Those ideals acted as a critique of the decisions of the powers. The same ideals proved uncomfortable for a Church with a dominant position in society; in order to justify its power and its inertia it had good reason to separate heaven from earthly time and to rehabilitate ancient notions of natural and cosmic laws. Millenarist ideals rode so loosely in respect to cosmic fate, natural law and therefore contemporary political necessity that they tended to destabilise social relations. For a Church that had come to inspire and sometimes organise the secular powers, they were the incarnation of heresy—that is, non-submission to the interests of the powers that be.

If the foregoing hypothesis is correct, the separation of 'heaven' from earth, seen in the practical sense of the outlawing of millenarianism, did not result from a doctrine established from the start or the necessary interpretation of the Easter event; instead it was a consequence of the failure of the Christian Empire and Christianity in the management of our world. The failure of this rule in regard to the establishment of the dreamed-of brotherhood, plenty and freedom led to the banishment of heaven and to the denial to it of any other than a moral connection with this world. It became a form of personal compensation with no anticipation in chronological time. It was seen as something like an inverted form of our world, out of the reaction against the Church's failure to make our society a fore-taste of the Kingdom of God.

If we allow the absence of any relation between our history and heaven, then history is either under the influence of fate or the arena of human effort. Western practice tended in the second direction, for the West had proposed theories in which the future was an integral part of reflection. On the basis of the transformation of the means of production and therefore because of a real possibility of winning control of human history, German thinkers and Marx especially played a decisive part in the 'secularisation' of millenarianism. By giving it material foundations, they eliminated the Promise which henceforth lost its earthly reference. This secularisation arose from the break between history and 'heaven'. Marx and, more emphatically, Ernst Bloch, asserted that this dichotomy was to the profit of the ruling classes and that the Church was on the side of the exploiters. The break was apparent in the first version of the Church's social doctrine: the eschaton (heaven) played no part in it, for it was dominated by the concept of 'nature'. Hence the Church put forward an organic and futureless society, opposed to those Socialist utopias which were guilty of transgressing the unchanging divine order of the world. This teaching would have had no purchase had it not found its location in the space provided by the now radical separation between earth and heaven: in this view, history is the repetition of a constant order, and sin or evil is the transgression of that order. This social doctrine was oblivious to the early Christian millenarianism and underestimated the novelty of practice and ideas afforded by the industrial era; deprived of an eschatology, it reduced history to a natural phenomenon.

Though millenarist hopes revived in secular or political theories, para-doxically the Churches treated them with aversion, scenting in their desire to mould the world a whiff of Satanic competition for the position vacated by the Kingdom. It is possible, of course, that there was some degree of dislike for doctrines or practices which merely wrote out in a new form the age-old dream of the Church. Hence the radical separation between history and the eschaton (heaven), and the inverted form in which the beyond was henceforth conceived, expressed the Church's inability to realise in practice what it proclaimed, and to embody what it promised to be: and anticipation of the Kingdom.

2. A DIVIDED THEOLOGY AND THE NEW TESTAMENT EVALUATION

My hypothesis would seem to give us a clearer insight into some original tendencies in contemporary theology. I am thinking particularly of American process theology[4] and of Pohier's *Quand je dis Dieu*.[5]

These theologies have a dual aim: to avoid a commonly accepted eschatology that supports a wholly negative relation to our world and has destructive effects in Christian behaviour; and to reintroduce the eschaton (heaven) into our worldly time by acknowledging God's blessing on our world, and by engaging in the responsible struggle to ensure that human history should be moulded by men without the imperative of an antecedent divine order. In this project, the millenarian ideals are freed from any mythic or transcendent character and anticipate the eventual historical struggle in which men are the only agents, for God does not establish any programme of liberation. The Church neither mediates nor prophesies any kind of happy earthly future in or outside history; it bears witness to the bestowal now of the Spirit whereby we are asked to offer thanks to God the creator in our actual, and now no longer some dream-like, circumstances.

Whatever the quite various cultural arguments with which they support their systems, these theologies more or less explicitly take note of the inability of the Churches to enact the Promise and of the falsehood inherent in its relegation to a world beyond.

In spite of their daring and novelty, these theologies do not, I feel, break out of the circle established by the dichotomy which itself results from ecclesial impotence. They interpret the New Testament within this perspective of separation, as if it were obvious that New Testament thought had produced the 'history-eschaton' dichotomy, and conceive the celestial beyond on the lines of the inverted world idea. Thinking it impossible that the Church would ever make any positive, non-pathological and non-politically regressive connection between 'history and eschaton', they suppress one of the elements of the tension—the eschaton, and identify it with the existing relationship with God. In doing this, they are forced to see the apocalyptic projects of the Bible as a form of cultural excess, and discuss neither their origin nor their import. There is no longer any heaven in the beyond or on earth. There is human happiness; and any dream of a happiness that is more than human and goes so far as to oppose the rule of sin and death runs the risk of effects that are even more destructive than the absolute acceptance of our contingency and mortality.

There are several reasons for this theological reversal. The critiques emanating from psychoanalytical and Marxist circles are far from unconnected with this new interpretation. Nevertheless I am inclined to think that the resentment expressed and felt against the Church's powerlessness to put into practice what it proclaims as promised may play a considerable part in the cavalier attitude taken to certain essential aspects of the New Testament. Furthermore, the disappearance of the eschaton in favour of the present moment by reason of the absolute nature of death and because of contingency also directly affects the secular millenarianisms, especially that of Ernst Bloch, as much as it undermines the way in which for centuries the Churches have put forward 'heaven' as the ultimate goal of human calling and action.

These theologies have a defect: they criticise the notion of 'heaven' relegated to a place outside the conditions of its historical production.

Seen thus, it is an inversion of our present condition, which is therefore found inadequate when set against the imaginary ideal that can never be realised in the Church. 'Heaven' is set against chronological time, makes any attempt to mould it pure vanity, and encourages resignation and exploitation.

Nevertheless these theologies issue from a very real intuition: namely, that God's blessing is bestowed here and now; therefore it is in the here-and-now that the world is given to man as the location of his happiness. If the idea of a 'celestial heaven' effectively condemns this blessing, it follows that this 'heaven' contradicts the blessing of God on this world and God's intention that man should be humanly happy. A dream of blessedness that denigrates an already possible happiness is destructive.

Is this true perception opposed to the eschatological framework of the New Testament? Is it true that any dream which accords with the impulse of desire contradicts the possible enactment now of happiness? Is the prospect opened up by the New Testament really a dilemma: should we reject all present happiness and joy in order to enjoy a suprahuman or divine happiness and joy? Or should we just assume that there are limitations inherent in human happiness and reject the destructive power of the longed-for divine joy? The millenarianism of the early Christians assumed a naïve and mythic form of hope in a terrestrial era of freedom, brotherhood and plenty that would lead to the promised divine joy; it does not encourage us to see Christian eschatology in terms of the dilemma I have just described. But since the New Testament is our sole norm of judgment, we have to analyse its viewpoint.

It would be incorrect to interpret Christian eschatology by separating the Easter mystery (the death and resurrection of Jesus) from the way that he followed in his preaching and activity. That is the way which the Gospels testify to, and which determines the meaning of Good Friday and Easter. This way that Jesus followed is inseparable from the joyous news of the imminence of the Kingdom of God. When the disciples of John the Baptist (Mt. 11:2-6, Lk. 7:18-23) ask Jesus: 'Are you he who is to come, or shall we look for another?', Jesus answers by drawing on Isaiah: 'Go and tell John what you hear and see: the blind receive their sight and the lame walk, lepers are cleansed and the deaf hear, and the dead are raised up, and the poor have good news preached to them. . . .'

The chains are broken; to be 'saved' is to become full of the nearness of God. The key-word of this breaking of the bonds of fate is: 'Rise and walk' (Mt. 9:5). The miracles of Jesus are the frontline of this advance of the Kingdom, its very incandescence here below. Those who were quite defeated rise up. Jesus does not call the heroic to realise this hope; he brings the failing light to life.

The beatitudes are the paradoxical sign of this awakening of hope. There Jesus declares that those who are to all intents and purposes down are in fact the happy ones: the poor, the hungry, those who weep, the persecuted (Lk. 6:20-4). The poor have no power on earth, the hungry have no physical energy, those who weep are defeated and the persecuted no longer have peace. They are all people without hope and yet theirs is the Kingdom. It is not among the rich, the roisterers, the exploiters and the persecutors (Lk. 6:25-6), who are the unhappy and unfortunate.

Jesus does not preach inertia, as if it were necessary to wait for death and the world beyond. He says: there is no future for the exploiters, for those who make people weep and for those who persecute. Only the merciful and the tender-hearted, the peace-seekers and the pure in heart produce happiness (Mt. 5:7-11). It is not the laws of cosmic entropy or the iron laws of biology which decide in the last resort who shall 'inherit the earth' (Mt. 5:4). The beatitudes are primarily a declaration of revolt against those laws in accordance with which, in a sociological acceptance, might is right; if that were so, then the rich could exploit the poor mercilessly, and the powerful could make people weep and persecute them. But the rich and powerful forget that they make the earth uninhabitable; that they produce unhappiness. A heaven on earth? Yes, but that heaven will never be produced by the rule of power.

Jesus did not offer any apology for suffering; on the contrary, he firmly opposed it by exposing not the natural machinery of suffering but its human reasons: the hoarding of riches or domination to the extent that freedom disappears. Jesus did not ask men to love the cross but to bear it in a certain context—one which demanded a break with family bonds holding men to the past, or one suffused with fear of risking one's own life and thus rendering it impossible to build an appropriate future. Jesus did not ask men to separate the beyond from the here-and-now in some kind of inverted world process. There is no Kingdom or ultimate heaven that is not an extension of demonstrable aspects of this world.

Those theologians to whom the question of an ultimate heaven is a matter of indifference are right up to a point. If there is certainly a heaven it is anticipated here below, for man's chief end is to live in happiness. Therefore it is here and now that men live under God's blessing. God said that what he had done was good; and God does not repent of his creation. Jesus' Gospel does not reject any part of what the Old Testament articulated so emphatically that it showed no interest, throughout almost its entire history, in the question of any kind of life after death. What is important is that the faithful should be firmly and passionately attached to present happiness so that, by virtue of the great promises made, they do not in any way hold it light. Jesus did not withdraw anything of the strength and wholesome truth of the Old Testament; he did not build his

Gospel on liberation from our world, or on flight from the world, or on resignation. On the contrary, like Job, Jesus proclaimed the happiness of those who make others happy, and did so out of impatience with misfortune and out of rebellion against the multitude of oppressions which turn our world into a jungle. Jesus did not glorify tears, or hunger or the injustice men undergo; he spoke out against those who make others weep, who persecute and kill. In this sense, Jesus did not break with but fulfilled the prophetic tradition of Israel.

But the same theologians are wrong up to a point. They underestimate God's passionate concern for mankind. God's cause is men's happiness. God's intention is not mediocre, the more creative the object of his desire is, the more generous his intention. The bounds of the field of action God allows us are measured only by his passionate love. The theologians I have referred to tend to confine God as if they were privy to his counsel and knew more about his aims than the New Testament. They use human weakness as a yardstick for God's behaviour. They believe that an ultimate heaven is the product of our own frustrations and see in the dislike of this life shown by many Christians the effects of this extravagant promise of a future to which the unmanageable contradictions of our contingent existence are painlessly relegated. They see the notion of heaven as the unhazardous revenge of those who detested the hazardous happiness of this world. Such a heaven is not anticipated on earth, and is inimical to the idea of a heaven on earth and it is a heaven without any warranty in the New Testament. The non-quantifiable moments of intense happiness which evoke another realm are indications of a dimension in which God follows only his own desire. Irenaeus, though his imagery was naïve, was more judicious when he praised God for gradually acclimatising us to joy. Iranaeus understood well that happiness removes that fear of God which is the last trace in every Christian of the pagan concept of divinity.

If men make an effort to build a heaven on earth, they are not in any way building in despite of God—as long, of course, as it is a question of a heaven and not of a utopia which later reveals its infernal countenance. God does not flourish by our misfortune; he rejoices when we rebel against all the iron laws of fate, whether natural or social. The desire to bring about happiness is a desire of the Gospel. If forms of belief in an eschatology after death encourage contempt for all personal, social, cultural or political effort to bring about happiness, to that extent they are to be assessed as non-Christian. The ancient form of millenarianism is not without meaning for us. It is outdated in form, and its imagery is naïve, but its hope is lasting. Not to separate earth and heaven is as valid an intention now as it was then. That separation works in favour of the privileged and reduces the oppressed to a state of resignation. The removal of all tension between an ultimate horizon and our present existence runs the long-term risk of separating men from their present life and of excluding the creative power of hope. It is the hope within the glow of a utopian future that energises the thrust towards happiness. It was because there was a promised land that Israel freed itself from slavery and the domination of the Egyptians. The New Testament places us in that tension; it does not reject the earthly heaven and it does not impose a heaven on us (for that would be contradictory), but it does articulate certain conditions. All forms of negation—no heaven on earth, no heaven with God—seem to me unfaithful to the direction of the New Testament.

Translated by John Griffiths

Notes

1. Iranaeus of Lyons *Adversus Haereses* L. V & 31-5 (ET: *Against Heresies* (London 1857)).
2. Origen *De Princ.* II, XI, 2; *P.G.,* XI, 241; Augustine *City of God* XX, vii.
3. Eusebius of Caesarea *Historia Ecclesiastica* L, X.
4. Ewert H. Cousins (Ed.) *Process Theology* (New York 1971).
5. J. Pohier *Quand je dis dieu* (Paris 1977).
6. Ernst Bloch *Atheismus im Christentum* (Frankfurt a.M. 1968).

Stephen Happel

The Structures of Our
Utopial *Mitsein* (Life-together)

IN *Portrait of the Artist as a Young Man,* James Joyce records what was surely part of an eschatology preached to most Christians of the previous generation:

> *Hell has enlarged its soul and opened its mouth without any limits*— words taken, my dear little brothers in Christ Jesus, from the book of Isaias. . . .
> Now, let us try for a moment to realise, as far as we can, the nature of that abode of the damned which the justice of an offended God has called into existence for the eternal punishment of sinners. Hell is a strait and dark and foulsmelling prison, an abode of demons and lost souls, filled with fire and smoke. . . . Boundless extension of torment, incredible intensity of suffering, unceasing variety of torture—this is what the divine majesty, so outraged by sinners, demands. . . .[1]

Although contemporaries readily reject the reprehensible use of psychological force in such texts, and make 'liberal' adjustments in the content, it is no longer simply a matter of the content that is in question. What is at issue is the very form of using images in our faith about the classical 'four' last things. Here the problem of form (image) and content (a spatialised eschatology at a future date) have become strictly correlative, and the problems of believing in a specific eternal life (either of bliss or punishment) are closely tied to the inclusion or exclusion of material images in our expressions of faith.

Although this essay cannot address all the particular re-interpretations of Christian eschatology available, it will indicate some of the conditions under which these representations might be critically appropriated by

Christian believers. Under what conditions might one give oneself to images of a future heaven, either those which have become part of our cultural past or those which might be formulated in the future? By ascertaining what some of those necessary (but not sufficient) conditions are, one will also achieve some knowledge about the world. Although this essay must concentrate primarily upon eschatological images, I believe Schubert Ogden is correct when he remarks that 'the problems of eschatology are really the problems of theology generally and the key to their solution is that particular form of faith in the reality of God which Christian theology is charged with making clear and explicit'.[2] The following examination, however, will reveal some significant differences in the approach to a solution.

1. CLASSICAL CHRISTIAN ESCHATOLOGY: SOME PROBLEMS

Death, (Particular and General), Judgment, Heaven, Hell (Limbo, Purgatory), the 'four' last things have recently found themselves in need of re-examination. Not only do theologians continue to criticise 'popular' notions of eschatology, but popular consciousness itself finds some ambiguity concerning these images. Each appears as too distinctly static, too individualist in execution, too singular in achievement, and only incipiently communal in the cosmological extravaganza called the general judgment. It is not that these interpretations of the eschaton in their more gentle moments have proven absolutely ineffective vehicles of faith; but that in the breakdown of classicist culture for which they were at once interpreter, critic, and component, they no longer prove effective for just those roles.[3] As other anthropologies emerge and the reflected experience of the Church accumulates, the images of classicist culture prove to be only one interpretation of the biblical and patristic texts. So theologians and preachers more frequently interpret death as a liminal experience, working its 'perishing' upon individuals throughout their lives; heaven and hell have shifted from their more cosmological expressions to interpretations stressing personal immediacy and personal deprivation. And particular judgment, like existence before death, must be communally situated.

Although these adjustments have been helpful in transition, the images themselves are likely to 'die a death of a thousand qualifications', unless one recognises that the whole complex is in need of re-formulation and re-interpretation. Are images of faith in heaven valid at all? How does one give oneself to such expressions authentically? Should the eschatological images which have charter significance for the Judeo-Christian tradition (e.g. Is 65:17-25 or Apoc 21) be forgotten precisely because of their strongly physical imagery? Some have not thought so; for example, Samuel Taylor Coleridge believed that to 'spiritualise' the eschatological texts destroyed the empirical character of Christian belief and undermined the historical revolution believers await.[4] But under what conditions might such images be authentically included in the beliefs of a faithful and thoughtful community? There are both theological and anthropological areas of discussion. I shall outline six.

2. ANTHROPOLOGY AND THE IMAGES OF HEAVEN

Temporality. If the Christian representations of eschatology are to be allowed some weight in determining a material future, then human experience of time must be 'de-spiritualised'. For much of Christian language about heaven, in spite its graphic detail in popular preaching, has gravitated toward the notion of a personal immortality of the spiritual soul. As Pannenberg remarks, the Greek notion of immortality of the soul provided a useful way to describe the interim state between individual death and the Second Coming and general Resurrection.[5] But what was useful in a classicist culture as a means of preserving spirit as consciousness, explaining personal perdurance, and maintaining a particular cosmology, fails to account for a strong contemporary sense of the physical character of subjectivity. To preserve the meaning of personal 'spirit', one postponed the enfleshed character of this finite until the 'end-times'. This combinative approach to immortality and resurrection of the body made itself felt in this life as well. Human temporality too quickly separated spirit as 'true' being from matter. But if the pictorial elements of Christian eschatology are to be taken seriously, then an anthropology which treats human temporality as spatial is essential. There is no human endeavor from the least perceptual operation to the most abstractive conceptualisation which is not material. Human time-consciousness is 'enfleshed'; even the reflections upon human operations ultimately involve representation.

Nor can this temporality be separated from the physical surrounding-world. For although one might find Origen's spiritualisation of cosmology a characteristically classicist solution to the experience of redeemed time, and Teilhard de Chardin's inclusions of physics and biology too 'poetic', both understood a 'human' temporality which did not exclude from redemption the world beyond other subjects.

To assert that the characteristic human movement is always a material dialectic is not to deny either a specific human subjectivity or a teleology. There is little doubt that if an anthropology must integrate the material at all levels to account for the pictorial content of eschatological images, that same anthropology must have some articulated *telos*. The question of an 'issue' to history must appear also in the case of the individual. Does history have an 'end'? If it does, then surely evidence for such an end is at least proleptically available in the teleology of individual subjectivity. The 'summing-up' of one's own time, and its relationship to others' estimations of one's goal-direction, execution and completion are neither irrelevant nor ignorant projects.

Images. Christian eschatology seems to require as a condition for its validity an anthropology which describes and explains the utterly physical/material character of subjectivity and its teleology. A part of that anthropology would require an investigation into the role of images in reality-formation, interpretation, and reformulation. It must account for the differences between image in perception, the representation by image in the absence of a perceived object, and those imaginative representations which function in art as interpretive of new meaning.

Perception is not simply a passive impression, but an achievement. To perceive an object as an identity through different moments requires both a reality which is conscious of the same and the similar through change and the varying aspects appearing in kinesthetic sense which delineate an identity. It is a subjectivity which perceives varying aspects, understands those aspects as indications of an object or class previously outlined, and judges this item to be this particular 'thing'. The case of an ambiguous presence is instructive. Should I not be clear concerning what it is that I am 'seeing', I 'run through' possible determinations of the presence (a tree? lamp-post? glowering giant? etc.); in determining a thing to be 'this particular thing', I determine that which fits both the data of sense and of interpretation. But image has played a crucial role in the setting of boundaries.

Pictures of those we love remain with us as presences, though the individual or group may be geographically distant or existentially absent. 'The peculiarity of pictorial presencing and representation is that pictures do not merely refer to something, but make that something present.'[6] One sees a particular presence in a picture, not simply a sign of that presence elsewhere.

In the creation of art-objects, whether there is or is not an original object from which the aesthetic artifact is modelled, what occurs is a taking of the environment of artifact as it is represented as an interpretation and presencing of the world. Through a play, a musical piece, or a painting, although it is the subject who now 'sees' the world in a new way, the world *is* now that way. The validation of such images of the world occurs in their continuing ability to interpret authentically the complex we call the human situation. Images then are crucial to the presencing, re-presencing, and doubling of the subject's temporality.

Utopia. Images of an idealised future occupy a special role within this investigation. Janus-like, utopias function as both critic of the present and past, and interpreter of future temporality. It is in validating the status of such images that one can provide the anthropological conditions for believing in images of heaven.

In the founding classic in the genre, Thomas More has his narrator argue that speculative philosophy is not suitable for all occasions. The world is not (cannot be?) totally rational; and therefore, pure rational argument will neither completely explain the present world, nor change it in the future. One has two choices, either to 'abandon the common-wealth' (silence) or to chose another mode of discourse. 'You must strive to guide policy indirectly, so that you make the best of things, and what you cannot turn to good, you can at least make less bad.'[7] The description of Utopia which follows, an *exemplum* within persuasive discourse, allows the reader to achieve an identity with a future which can only be incompletely realised through imagination.

Indeed, such a representation is necessary for accomplishing any future. The experience of the present is of a socio-economic reality which is not utterly good. Technological planning has proven insufficient to the tasks of achieving even the minimal cancellation of certain 'recalcitrant irrationalities', such as scarcity and war.[8] Moreover, the means toward the good have become tainted. Utopial visions offer a way of re-examining priorities. But what is their structure and status?

Utopias function within the society of their origin as a social critique.[9] Thus Utopial vision and satiric criticism are closely linked, and the truth of each is not unrelated to the present experience of the reader. Frequently, both satire and utopia agree in their criticisms of the contemporary society, but utopia offers a positive representation beyond the negation. So, for example, it is extraordinarily difficult to piece together what concrete society the acerbic wit of Jonathan Swift might envision on the other side of his criticisms in *Gulliver's Travels* (even the Houyhnmhnms are objects of laughter); yet in *Utopia,* there are broad outlines of an interlocking set of positive goods envisaged as possible. Utopial images, by their very nature, contain both this positive and negative comment.

Moreover, this social criticism functions as the locus for an important recognition concerning subjectivity. The form which irony takes in utopia and satire limits the present situation, and requires individual and society to distance themselves from their own productions.[10] The ironic doublings of the reader with the Yahaos and Houyhnmhnms or the Utopians do not lift the reader out of history, but rather create a history wherein consciousness successively outlives itself.

Because utopias direct themselves to both consciousness and to the content of socio-political endeavours, they operate in both a formal and material way. The image itself is a claim upon both social change and upon the individual/group to accomplish that change—an 'indirect' claim, as More says, but a claim nonetheless. The logic of utopia is subjunctive and conditional: If one would ... then; or optative: Why not? What if ...? Both More and perhaps more trenchantly Swift realise that the key to the presence of utopial vision is in the choice by the reader. 'For it is impossible to do all things well unless all men are good, and this I do not expect to see for a long time.'[11] The demand of the text upon the reader is an ethical one. The doubling of consciousness is a teleological conscience.

This ethical claim is in one sense a formal demand—and insistent assurance that the world could be otherwise than it is; but the exposition is always in terms of the information and techniques of control available in the present.[12] Thus the exact content of More's *Utopia* appears outdated with the passage of the technology which gave it birth. Yet certain social structures (e.g. education, sexual order, property management, domestic arrangements, etc.) appear as constant components in the tradition of utopias; and in each case, the utopial vision makes a formal ethical claim upon consciousness. Thus the truth of the claim depends upon the continuing perdurance of human choice and upon the continuing re-interpretation of social and personal structures of behaviour. The truthfulness of the contents of a vision of the future depends upon its progressive incarnation through human choice.

The intrinsic value of utopial vision is that it not only provides concrete goals for a given society but it also challenges to the realisation of those goals by its ironic comment upon the agent and the agent's behaviour. It is a fundamentally spatial interpretation of a common temporality. Indeed, it can be argued that the refusal to give oneself to an image of the future is a refusal to accept self-construction or construction of one's world and the projection of the self into an unknown. Utopial vision is possible achievement in the future dependent upon enactment through present choice.

3. THEOLOGY AND THE IMAGES OF HEAVEN

To speak about human issues in such a way is also to speak about God. If we are to understand under what anthropological conditions heaven may remain a truthful word within Christian vocabulary, then we must be aware that it requires some re-thinking of our notion of God. However, because this essay is most concerned about finding an 'anthropological grammar' for the Christian vocabulary about heaven, the specifically theological issues must be even more severely schematised. They centre around God, Christ, and the nature of religious experience.

God. If human temporality is to be understood spatially, then it will be necessary to re-think, to re-image our notions of God. The validity of eschatological images: the kingdom, the heavenly city, messianic feast, agricultural abundance, etc. is ultimately dependent upon their inclusion within the Divine. Rahner argues that the mysteries of eschatological fulfilment are the mystery of God Himself—but not a God who is divorced from the transformation of this world.[13] The autonomy of divine self-bestowal, the sovereignty of God in creation and redemption has been preserved in classicist culture by the argument that God is pure spirit. But this achievement (largely) of Origen was not an unmixed blessing for theology; for, although this interpretation established the contingency of matter, it also created a Divinity to whom it is difficult to 'attribute' concrete 'action'. To re-examine this most basic question in theology is imperative, if the contents of religious image are to be appropriated by the believer as unsurpassable and inexhaustible. In this re-examination, it might prove illegitimate to conceive of divine 'eternity' as a spaceless, indeed non-chronological, time in which static motionless 'experience' takes the place of history. While 'eternal life' may very well not be simply a prolongation of the present temporality, it cannot be irrespective of it. If this world as we know it is not irrelevant to that life within God, then it must be included within, rather than alongside, the Divine.

Christ. If the divine must be re-imaged, recognised as encompassing a transformed human spatio-temporal existence rather than cancelling it, then it is surely the Christian incarnation which permits such an assertion to be entertained while avoiding both pantheism and polytheism. It is not another God who became historical, but the one God. The history of this world is in some mysterious way the teleology of God himself. That is why the continuing exegesis of the resurrection of Jesus is crucial to what that transformed temporality is. Images of the future, if they are to be Christian must always include reference to that one event.[14] For it is the death-resurrection which is an event which is at once historical (in the sense of spatio-temporally empirical) *and* divine, not only indicating that the two are not exclusive, but that ultimately all past or future creation is to be interpreted in precisely this fashion. The mystery of the images of an end-time are mysteries of intra-Trinitarian life.

The Christian argues that concrete images of heavenly transformation have some real bearing on the empirical future of the world—because that future is also God's future. Therefore the hopes which the Christian has for this world and for final transformation are fundamentally intertwined. The Cross-resurrection brings all human structures under criticism, but it also argues that it is precisely *this* world which is God's history.

Religious Experience. Theologians frequently appeal to the tradition of mysticism when speaking of the purely spiritual, largely individual, and indeed unmediated relation of the individual with God. So the author of the *Cloud of Unknowing* asserts that the highest state of consciousness is to be 'nowhere': 'For myself, I prefer to be lost in this nowhere, wrestling with this blind nothingness, than to be like some great lord travelling everywhere and enjoying the world as if he owned it.[15] It seems, at least on the surface, that this experience of the mystic contradicts the argument that all temporality is image-laden and spatial. Yet when the mystics describe their ecstatic experience of God, the images used to describe this 'non-linguistic' experience, whether sexual, athletic, or gustatory, always seem heavily sense-laden. Would it not be better to explain the experience of awareness of God as always mediated, and in its highest moments a sense that one's entire subjectivity is an artifact of the divine? All the techniques of prayer and asceticism become partially progressive choices toward this one eschatological event in which self and world appear as the artwork of God. This doesn not deny ecstasy, but re-inserts its explanation into a spatial temporality. Life becomes not so much a matter of escaping images in religious experience, but of choosing the appropriate one. The Christian trusts in the *eikon* of Jesus the Christ; and the humanity of the resurrected Christ remains as the one mediation between the divine and human.

To summarise what has been outlined thus far: (1) it is possible to adjust the various eschatological images of the Christian 'end', but that does not direct us to the central question: the validity of images and their physical content in our relation with God; (2) there are definite anthropological conditions which would need to be articulated if images are to be recognised as a valid moment in religious language; and (3) there are correlative theological re-interpretations necessary for determining the validity of our ordinary images about heaven.

4. AN ALTERNATIVE MODE OF FUTURE: NEW CHRISTIAN SYMBOLS?

Christians are not, of course, the only community to describe the future. The Church's attempts to revise its notions of the future and the future of the world parallel those of Marxists and futurologists. There are those who introduce a note of discord into the harmonies of self-description by arguing that the diminishing resources of the world or the inherent self-destructive impulse of the species will produce catastrophe; but the everyday world continues without much attention to such apocalypse. Science fiction literature provides a more intriguing field for discovery of alternative symbols for the Christian heaven. Recent science fiction, as an agent of secular prophecy, has taken seriously More's remarks about ethical imperatives, and tried to redescribe extraterrestrial or intra-terrestrial utopial communities based upon various ethically perfect inter-subjectivities. Indeed, it is not commonplace to state that when scientific events began to rival fictional description in the 1960's, science fiction transferred its attention to interior criteria for achievement of the 'good life'. Although intermediate beings in the universe (secularised angels and saints) still perform the function of education or idealisation in narrative, it is not so much new technological advances that are taught poor mortals, but new ways of 'being-with' one another. It is such a shift toward the 'structures of *being-with*' which has charmed the hearts of the young (Heinlein's *Strangers in a Strange Land*) and re-injected a note of the 'mysterious explanation' into popular culture (*Chariots of the Gods, Close Encounters of the Third Kind*). It is the social, utopial structures revealing inter-subjectivity which appear as a fruitful area for the re-interpretation of Christian heaven.

This offers two broad cultural motifs within which Christianity should re-examine its images of eschatology: utopia and inter-subjectivity. In each area, previous cultural syntheses, largely bourgeois, individualist, or 'spiritualising' in shape, will give way to a sense of the inter-dependence of beings and the societal character of images.

First then, because the enactment of a social utopia is a truth contingent upon human choice, we are informed by it of three important features of Christian heaven: (1) visions of heaven are likely to address themselves primarily to the explicit lack in humanly constructed utopias (for example, the hiatus between knowledge of the true and the enactment of the good); (2) the concrete content of heavenly utopias will cast themselves in terms of the social/individual constants of human behaviour; and (3) the truthfulness of these constants as goals will not be irrespective of human choice in the present. None of these elements seem outside the realm of the biblical images.

Secondly, as we have noted, an emphasis on inter-subjectivity is not foreign to previous Christian descriptions of 'eternal life'. The essence of mystical contemplation remains the structured encounter between a divine and human subject. Consciousness of God is indeed the encounter with primordial negativity, the recognition that the divine subject is inexhaustibly present, and that the finite subject is so because of its life within the other. But the only way for this personal mysterious horizon to be present is through figure. The recognition of the simultaneity of figure and ground most profoundly characterises mystical awareness.

This 'seeing of God', need not appear as a static experience; rather it becomes the eternally active self-bestowal by the divine in Christ and the progressive self-adherence to this one Image of God. Because the other is infinite subjectivity, the falling-in-love with love itself is progressive, and is ever in process of achievement, involving continuous transformation of the finite subject, an anticipatory movement into love without anxiety or possible loss of presence. For the Christian, this falling-in-love with God means adherence to Christ; one's adherence to Christ continues, now transformed into ever deeper and more complex involvement.

It is in this context of a mutual divine-human love that the inter-connectedness of finite subjectivities is achieved. Although the claims made by utopial visions must depend upon individuals' willingness to change in the present, such visions define a social body. In so far as a social group activates the content-claims of utopias, it constitutes itself as something beyond an agglomerate—it becomes a community, sharing common goals, common means, and enacting common meaning. The common meaning in this case is Christ, and the community is his Church.

The 'new' symbols of heaven will look remarkably like those 'charter-images' of the Scriptures. Besides the simple fact that new meanings are always broken from old languages, the structures of 'being-with' perdure, however transformed, through cultural change. As a result, the images of Is 65 or Apoc 21 continue to validate themselves in the context of the City, natural abundance, or inter-species non-violence. The appropriate attitude to the content of the 'old' images is not complete rejection, but re-interpretation—the continuing validation of Christian hopes.

For there are always two foci to the Christian case for the future. In each image: the perfect city, the kingdom, the peaceful, fruitful country-side, 'being-with' without violence and with care, the central fact for the Christian is this coming experience as gift and mystery. Each image is within the self-bestowal of God; each, while contingent upon the ethical choices of finite subjects, is at the same time the primordial achievement of God. That is, in fact, a central assertion of the images of heaven and parousia—that all human enactments require criticism, revision, and re-enactment—and that this process is within God. The Christian's plans for the future are always concrete, yet always revisable, constantly offering new programmes to enact heavenly vision, while always criticising offered projections.

By both form and content, therefore, images of heaven have a legitimate place in Christian religious (and in human) discourse. In form, they recall the Christian community to the absolute task of absolute self-revision; in content, they constantly re-incarnate the fundamental *Mitsein* ('being-with') which is at the basis of all human interchange—the choice of God to 'be with' us.

Notes

1. J. Joyce *Portrait of the Artist as a Young Man* edited by C. G. Anderson (New York 1968) pp. 117, 119, 131. Note that Joyce only slightly adapted this text from an existing model.

2. S. Ogden *The Reality of God* (New York 1966) p. 210.

3. For the distinction between classicist culture and a culture founded in historical consciousness, see B. J. F. Lonergan 'Theology in its New Context' in *Second Collection* edited by W. F. J. Ryan and B. J. Tyrell (London 1974) pp. 55-67.

4. See, for example, Coleridge's remarks in BM Add. MS. 47524 (NB 26), fol. 69v. [ca. 1827]; or BM Add. MS. 47536 (NB 41), fols. 12v.-13 [1829].

5. W. Pannenberg *The Apostles' Creed* (London 1972) p. 171 ff.

6. R. Sokolowski 'Picturing' *The Review of Metaphysics* 31 (Sept. 1977), 21. Throughout this section, this article has proven extraordinarily helpful.

7. T. More *Utopia* translated and edited by H. V. S. Ogden (New York 1949) p. 23. Compare the remark of J. Swift *Gulliver's Travels* (Boston 1960) p. 226 about the need for 'exhortation' so that reason may truly operate.

8. See for this entire discussion T. R. Flynn 'The Use and Abuse of Utopias' *The Modern Schoolman* 53 (1976) 241.

9. This point is commonly made, but for a recent re-interpretation and 'reconstruction' of the social text upon which *Utopia* comments, see L. Marin *Utopiques: Jeux d'Espaces* (Paris 1973) and an interpretation by Fredric Jameson 'Of Islands and Trenches: Naturalisation and the Production of Utopian discourse' *diacritics* 7 (1976) 2-21.

10. S. Kierkegaard *The Concept of Irony* translated by L. M. Capel. (Bloomington, Ind. 1968) p. 338 ff.

11. T. More *Utopia* p. 23; compare J. Swift *Gulliver's Travels* p. 190.

12. See the discussion of utopial antinomies, and whether utopias are 'fully rationalised' in G. Bonnet 'Intentions Ethiques de l'Utopie' *Supplément* 119 (Nov. 1976) 517-48.

13. K. Rahner 'Marxist Utopia and the Christian Future of Man' *Theological Investigations* Vol. 6, translated by K. H. and B. Kruger (Baltimore 1969) p. 59. Similar points are also made by G. Vahanian *God and Utopia* translated by P. Lachance *et. al.* (New York 1977).

14. K. Rahner 'The Hermeneutics of Eschatological Assertions' *Theological Investigations* Vol. 4, translated by K. Smyth (Baltimore 1966) pp. 342-3.

15. The *Cloud of Unknowing* edited by W. Johnston (New York 1973) pp. 135-37. See the classic commentary, J. Marechal *Studies in the Psychology of the Mystics* translated by A. Thorold. (New York 1964) pp. 194-5, 198, 200.

Contributors

AELRED CODY, OSB, priest-monk of St Meinrad Archabbey, was born in 1932 in Oklahoma City (USA). Doctor of Theology (Ottawa) and of Holy Scripture (Rome), Diplômé de l'École Biblique et Archéologique de Jérusalem, Associate of the Royal Colleges of Music and of Organists (London), he has been professor of Holy Scripture in St Meinrad Seminary (Indiana, USA) and, since 1968, in Rome (Sant' Anselmo; the Pontifical Biblical Institute). Among his publications are *Heavenly Sanctuary and Liturgy in the Epistle to the Hebrews,* 1960; *A History of Old Testament Priesthood,* 1969; and various articles in the main international scriptural journals.

JAMES H. CONE is the Charles A. Briggs' Professor of Systematic Theology at the Union Theological Seminary in New York, USA. He was born in 1938 in Fordyce, Arkansas, and completed his formal education at Northwestern University (Ph.D.). He is best known for having written the first book on black theology entitled *Black Theology and Black Power* (1969). He is also the author of three additional books: *The Spirituals and the Blues* (1972); *A Black Theology of Liberation* (1970); *God of the Oppressed* (1975).

CHRISTIAN DUQUOC, OP, was ordained in 1953. He teaches dogmatic theology in the Theological Faculty of Lyons University and is a member of the Editorial Board of the journal *Lumière et Vie.* Among his major works are the two volumes of a *Christologie* (Paris 1972).

ROBERT FAVRE was born in Lyon in 1927. Educated at The École Normale Supérieure, he taught in Algiers then in Lyon where he is currently lecturer in French Literature at the University. His publications include *Les Memoires de Trévoux* and papers on medicine; he has contributed to *XVIIIe siècle,* the three series of *Etudes sur la presse* and *Dictionnaire des Journalistes. 1600-1789.*

STEPHEN HAPPEL was born in Indianapolis, Indiana in 1944. He holds graduate degrees in philosophy, literary criticism, and most recently in theology completing a dissertation *with Professor Walgrave* at Louvain (KUL) on the role of imagination in religious discourse. At present, he teaches systematic theology at St Meinrad School of Theology, St Meinrad, Indiana.

JAN KERKHOFS was born in Hasselt on 15 May 1924. He entered the Society of Jesus in 1942 and was ordained priest in 1956. He studied at Louvain, Münster and Oxford. He is a licentiate in philosophy and theology and has a doctorate in sociology. He teaches pastoral sociology in the Faculty of Theology of the Catholic University of Louvain. He is also the Secretary General of the international centre for study and information Pro Mundi Vita at Brussels. He is the spiritual advisor to UNIAPAC International.

RENÉ LUNEAU was born at Nantes in France in 1932. He is a Dominican, a reader in theology and a doctor of literature. He also holds a diploma of the École Pratique des Hautes Etudes (Paris) and an engineering diploma of the Centre Nationale de la Recherche Scientifique. He teaches at the Institut Catholique in Paris. He has written a thesis on marriage and the position of women in rural Mali. He has also published, in collaboration with L. V. Thomas, who teaches at the Sorbonne, several works on the traditional religions of black Africa. Together with C. Geffré, he was responsible for the number of *Concilium* devoted to the future of the African churches (No. 126).

JAN NELIS was born in Haarlemmerliede in 1919 and was ordained priest in 1946 as a member of the Congregation of the Blessed Sacrament. Between 1947 and 1950, he studied at the Pontifical Biblical Institute and the École Biblique in Jerusalem. He graduated in 1975 at the Catholic University of Nijmegen, where he has been teaching Old Testament exegesis since 1965. His publications include translations of and commentaries on Daniel (Roermond 1954); Job, together with C. Epping (Roermond 1968); I and II Maccabees (Roermond 1972 and 1975), and many articles in *Bijbels Woordenboek, Catholica* and *Theologisch Woordenboek*.

JUAN LUIS RUIZ DE LA PEÑA was born in Asturias in 1937, and ordained priest in 1961. He received his doctorate in theology from the Gregorian in 1970 and lectures in Systematic Theology at the Pontifical University of Salamanca. His publications include: *El hombre y su muerte: Antropología teológica actual* (Burgos 1971); *La otra dimensión. Escatología cristiana* (Madrid 1975); *Muerte y marxismo humanista* (Salamanca 1978).

PETER STOCKMEIER was born in 1925 in Hemhof, near Rosenheim, Upper Bavaria. After military service he studied theology and history in Munich until 1952, and gained his doctorate there in 1955. He has taught Church History in the Universities of Triev and Tübingen. Since 1 October 1969 he has been full professor and holder of the chair of Early Church History, Patrology and Christian Archaeology at the Institute for Church History of the University of Munich.